JUN 1 1 2021

HOW TO DISCUSS POLITICS ONLINE

Stop Falling for %$!#@ Marketing Tactics!*

KATHERINE YOUNG

This book goes out to everyone who tries to do better every day and tries to show up as their best selves when discussing politics online.

I see you and you make a difference.
You can't change anything without intention.

And to Angie, thank you for your support and listening to me go on and on about this book project for years.

Table of Contents

Chapter 3
HOW TO SEE MARKETING TACTICS

Chapter 4
THAT DOESN'T MEME WHAT YOU
THINK IT MEMES 89

CHAPTER 1

ONLINE POLITICAL CONVERSATIONS TODAY

1.1 Our Online Experience Needs Changing

With our smartphones always within an arm's reach continually logged into social media, we simply cannot take for granted the impact of the content we consume and post on those platforms. Over the past few years we have all watched how unethical content created for social platforms has spread.

Political commentators and trolls are churning out divisive content at an exponential rate with immeasurable impact. There is no longer a learning curve with meme generating technology, and anyone can create divisive content with the sole purpose of validating their need to feel significant. These people are changing the way we think and see the world through propaganda and marketing tricks.

This new breed of unethical Internet marketer is now able to reach a wide audience with very little technical skill and is challenging the limits of our first amendment rights. They have shown us that biased content can influence culture and our ability to solve problems effectively when divided. With our attention span growing ever shorter, the outlandish content grows louder.

Freedom of speech has never meant freedom from consequences. Everything you say or post online can have a consequence, and our country is dealing with the consequences of the new language of division that has been successfully marketed to all of us online. This content has affected us all and it is time for us to take responsibility for what our online environments have become. What has happened can't be blamed solely on the media or politicians, because much of it is our own fault. We are the ones who have shared this content without a second thought of the ramifications of our actions. We post truly hateful content, reading into it what we want it to say, and our actions have clearly extended beyond the screen. We are a divided country now more than ever before in modern history.

All of us consume social media in one way or another. And you can pretty much assign all social media users into two groups: those who are almost silent, and those who are screaming. This book is written for both. We need people to have real conversations online again—conversations that include listening and not oversimplifying topics into who's right and who's wrong. It isn't politics that causes bad reactions; it is the marketing and the divisive content we share that creates the problems.

We need those who have the silent strategy to speak up. We need to hear your thoughts. You have to take responsibility for what you didn't say that you should have. Your silence is allowing the extremes to be amplified, allowing lies to continue to spread unchallenged, and is making you an accomplice to the problem.

And we need those of you who are screaming to be smarter about what you post and to see the division and marketing tactics it employs. We need you to stop posting videos, divisive memes, and 'facts' that are complete bullshit. We all need to use our words like big kids and take responsibility instead of just reposting someone else's overly simplified opinion on a political topic.

This book is a call to action for both types to step up and not simply rely on your fight or flight responses. Real conversations take actual effort and I am requesting that we all be more mindful when approaching politically polarizing issues online. We need thoughtful conversation, personal experiences, and a willingness to listen. We do not need to repost a troll's idea over and over and we certainly don't need one more video telling anyone 'the truth' to make ourselves feel superior. This book will show you how such marketing tactics are used to make you like and share and the damage they cause. It is time to take responsibility and turn things around. It is time to do better.

1.2 See Social Media Through A Marketer's Lens

This book will help you see content online like a marketer. I have over a decade of experience in social media marketing, graphic design, and communications, and have run social media accounts for large companies like the Walt Disney Company, and for other clients in the communications, education, and nonprofit fields. I also run my own artist accounts and have created viral content that has spread worldwide. I have seen firsthand the global impact of one single image that was created in minutes. My experience turns memes and posts into marketing tactics and I am going to help you see it through the eyes of a marketer.

Some people hear the word marketing and think it sounds complex, some people think it is irrelevant to them, but it is neither. Marketing is anything that makes people think a certain way or have a certain response; and it's sole purpose isn't just to sell things. It can also make people believe in a political opinion or in logic that is actually deceptive. Historically there has always been a battle between marketers and consumers. Marketers try new tricks to outsmart consumers, and then consumers become smarter and no longer fall for their tricks. The tactics now used by marketers have moved so fast that consumers haven't caught up. We are falling for fake news and spreading divisive content being marketed to us. It is time to level the playing field. I will show you the tactics behind online content and hopefully help you become a more savvy digital consumer. I have made many mistakes and I have my own biases, but I hope with the help of this book you will be able to move forward with a better understanding of how we are all being marketed to online.

1.3 What the Heck Am I Talking About?

I am going to talk a great deal about divisive content, memes, and trolls. I am going to refer to these in a pretty broad context as defined below:

Divisive Content (noun)
A post online that is made primarily to point the finger at a group or individual to let them know they are in the wrong according to your subjective opinion, more so than to promote a cause you care about. You may think your post isn't divisive but it usually takes an opposing viewpoint to see it in the context it was truly meant for. These posts put negativity into the world instead of positivity when discussing political topics and let people know they are your enemy and you are against them.

Meme (noun)
A meme is a humorous or impactful image, video, piece of text, etc., that is copied (often with slight variations) and shared rapidly by Internet users.

Troll (noun and verb)

A troll is someone who wants attention for their thoughts online and goes about it by bullying, being divisive, and spreading misinformation to fit their agenda. They create most memes and are defined by their acts of online hatred. A troll can be anyone who displays this kind of behavior.

I will be using the words social media, online, and the Internet pretty interchangeably. This is because I think of social media as just the current condition of the Internet. There really isn't any place that you can't be heard if you want to be heard.

I will talk a great deal about marketers/marketing and consumers. I am using these terms in the broadest sense. Marketing or marketers are any action/person/ organization that is trying to elicit a response of some kind. You don't have to be paid to be marketing something. You simply want to garner a response. Consumers are anyone online who sees this content. Being a consumer doesn't mean you have to buy something. Your attention is enough to make you a consumer.

I am also going to use words like scream or yell and aggressive language; I am referring to the way you are coming across online when someone else sees the content you posted in their feed. Even if it is just words, they might be read as if you are yelling at someone because of the way it uses aggressive language. Anytime you are posting online you are talking not just typing. Please see the glossary for more defined terms.

1.4 Why is Understanding Meme Culture Important?

Today's society thrives on entertainment. Most homes have living rooms centered around a television with all kinds of streaming services connected to it and probably multiple televisions throughout the house. We binge watch TV shows, we take our sports team loyalty seriously, and we are obsessed with reality TV shows that glamorize bad behavior and the trope of the overnight success whose hidden talent was discovered. Add in our smartphones consistently within reach and you can see how many things are competing loudly for your time and attention.

Each of us has an attention filter that locates information that we find important out of all this noise. Most often dramatic stories, things that make us fearful, and information that aligns with our beliefs get through this filter. This competition for your attention has created an environment in which content must be simpler and more dramatic to get through your attention filter. Memes check all these boxes to get your attention. Hans Rosling does an amazing job at explaining how your attention filter works in his book *Factfulness*.

Memes leverage the KISS (Keep It Simple, Stupid) strategy to get your attention.

They take big ideas and boil them down to a simple dramatic concept. The problem is they usually leave out a ton of nuanced information or are false altogether—the fact that they got your attention is all that matters. And by doing this over and over again they are making these ideas anecdotally true.

It is now extremely easy to create content that looks fairly professional and upload it online for all to see. You don't need a radio station to start a podcast, a professional camera studio to post a video, a journalism degree to write and post your opinion, or a degree in graphic design to make a meme or alter an image. Creating a meme that gets a million+ shares is as easy as an app on your phone. This creates an environment where unethical and divisive content is side by side with actual news that takes time to read. . . and guess which one gets past our attention filter?

Check out these two memes that I created with information from GeneralMediaAssociation.org. The facts on the memes are all going to be true except for one. I guarantee you that it will be hard to pick out the false fact. Your own confirmation bias is going to make you far more likely to believe the ones that align with your side. These took me less than ten minutes to research and create and you have probably seen a ton of memes that are very similar.

1.4.1 This meme was made by the author in under ten minutes with information found at: GeneralMediaAssociation.org.

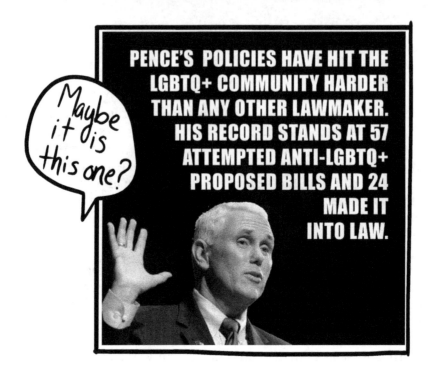

1.4.2 This meme was made by the author in under ten minutes with information found at: GeneralMediaAssociation.org.

So how did you do? Do you think you know which meme contains the false fact? Would you have known that one was false if I hadn't told you? The biggest problem with memes online is none of them have disclaimers stating,*This meme isn't true, but please share it as if it is fact. They all come from groups we are in, they are posted by family and friends we trust, and from webpages that sound official. We automatically give memes online more authority and credibility than they actually deserve because of the social credibility they have from being shared by sources we trust or appear trustworthy. Marketers know this.

Trolls feel more accomplished and more self-important the more likes and shares they get on a post, so they have far more incentive to create a meme that will go viral than a meme that is actually true. True content isn't flashy or as simple as right and wrong. And true content won't give them the attention they crave. So they keep creating what works and it doesn't have to be true to get them the attention they seek.

Bonus round: Did you actually take out your phone and check the facts listed on the memes or Google the General Media Association? Because if you did you will see the site isn't a real source. Because I lied to you. All those memes were pulled right from my rectal database. The GeneralMediaAssociation.org isn't even a real source. It is a website name I bought for $11.99 because I thought it sounded pretty legit. And nowhere did I have to prove I wasn't a nonprofit or a legitimate organization to make that site a .org site. There was no Internet police to stop me.

In this day in age with the collective knowledge of the world at the tip of your fingers, I believe you have an ethical obligation to check information before you share it with people who trust you. Because you are making a personal recommendation and that recommendation is the most powerful kind of marketing on the planet. You can stop the cycle of misinformation, and breaking that cycle is the most responsible thing you can do online.

1.4.3 The fake news cycle can be broken by fact-checking. If you don't fact-check memes, you contribute to the cycle of fake news spreading. Because of the personal recommendations behind the fake news we see over and over we trust it more than we should. When we don't see real news cover what we have been bombarded with by memes it builds suspicion that news isn't covering what it should be and our trust shifts to unreliable sources. We all need to take responsibility to break this cycle.

1.5 The Impact of One Image

No one truly knows the impact memes have had on our country's politics and on our population as a whole, however I have had an insider's look at just what a viral meme can do. And I am going to compare two viral memes to show just how big an impact these things can have.

In September 2016 I saw a meme comparing *Girls' Life* magazine next to *Boys' Life* magazine and I was so appalled I decided to do my own version of the *Girls' Life* magazine cover.

1.5.1 Original image posted to Facebook by Matt Frye that inspired me to create my own cover of the Girls' Life *magazine.*

1.5.2 The new cover idea spread around the world. It was shared by local and national news sources with the largest being the TODAY Show, the #1 morning show in the US.

1.5.3 The cover redo on the right went viral. It was created by me in less than ten minutes.

The post became a viral sensation. Celebrities chimed in on the conversation, I did interviews for media around the world, and the image was even featured on the TODAY show. And it had real lasting effects, including shifts in the magazine industry in how they represent women and girls and what topics they cover. There are now features across women's magazines highlighting strong women and I even inspired some incredible women to launch their own magazine in Malaysia. This all happened because of one meme made by one person. And it took me less than ten minutes to make!

And here is the kicker: The original Facebook post that went viral was shared less than 500 times. That one post reached 114,569 people. But that was just the original Facebook post. I saw posts online with 20,000+ shares and there is no way to know how many times this was shared and viewed around the world. But it was probably seen by millions of people with all the media coverage and also by people that shared the image on their own. This one image created a global conversation and it exploded past what I could possibly see. That is how virality works. Its impact with each share is multiplied. You may think of each share as an additional share, but really it is a multiplication of dozens or even hundreds causing a snowball effect.

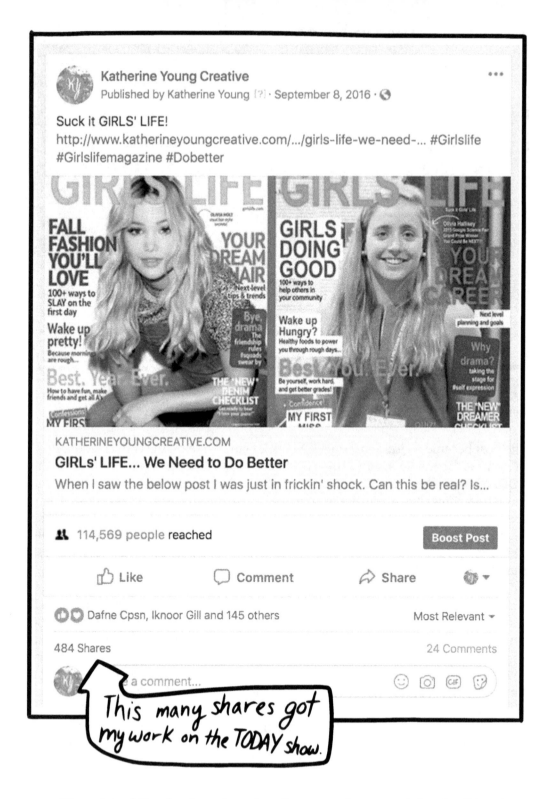

1.5.4 *The original Facebook post got less than 500 shares and that is all it takes to go internationally viral and make a huge impact on a global conversation.*

Now let's take a look at another meme. This meme is also from September 2016. It claims the coach said these horrible words. The coach never said these words as attributed in the post. And just this one post was shared almost 500,000 times! Almost 500,000 times!!!! Just this one meme. This doesn't even take into account all the memes where people took the image and wording without permission and shared it themselves. And thousands of fake memes just like this are constantly being created every day nonstop. There are also thousands of groups and troll profiles online that do nothing but spread this divisive and fake content all day everyday.

1.5.5 This one post and others like it spread like wildfire and their impact is immense. Can you believe none of these people bothered to check if it was real? It has a million interactions and 490,000+ shares. The impact of this is far greater than my one meme. And mine altered an industry.

I can't show you the behind the scenes number of how many people actually saw this post, but compared to my post this one has far more global population impact than mine according to the numbers. It was shared 1,000 times more than mine and a million people interacted with it! Just imagine how many people this one meme reached when compared to the reach of mine. This meme (or one imitating it) most likely was seen by someone in every single household in the United States and far beyond. It is terrifying at the least and alters history at the worst.

Fake and divisive content has tricked, impacted, and caused all of us to act on a scale we can't even admit to ourselves. And just comparing the impact and reach of two memes proves it. If you want to see these two memes compared more in-depth, check out my blog post: *Someone I Know Loves This Fake News*, where I break it down even further.

1.6 You are a Product

Wait what? Didn't I just explain how we are all consumers? Keep in mind that anytime you aren't paying for something, you are a product. Think about it. No one shares something online hoping no one sees it, no one likes it, and no one interacts with it. So we all give it our best effort to make sure people like what we create and post. That keeps us online and keeps our friends and family online too. The longer you are online the more money for ads platforms can charge. So if you are going somewhere online for free and not buying anything, remember just being there is making them money.

Algorithms figure out what to show you to keep you online longer. The more angry a publication's articles make you, the more a video makes you laugh, and the more memes you share with your friends, the longer you are online—the more money you are generating to all kinds of third parties. It is just that simple.

1.7 Target Markets

Anyone who knows me can testify that I just love all things Disney! Every time Disney comes out with something new, it feels like it was made just for me! Do you have something in your life that feels just like that? Something that feels like it was made for you? If so, thank marketing.

We all fall into groups that marketers call a target market. A target market is a group of people with similar interests, beliefs, or backgrounds. It makes you easier to sell to. It is easier to make something a few people really like than something all people will like. Despite all of us thinking we are completely unique, it really isn't the case when it comes to marketing tactics.

So when you see a meme or an article that you feel compelled to post, it is because it was created specifically for people like you. You are the target market for that content. It feels true and right to post because it was made to feel that way for people like you. They sold you an idea and you did exactly what they wanted you to do.

1.8 Instinctive Thinking vs. Adaptive Thinking

Have you ever gone to write an angry e-mail at work but then let yourself cool down and write it the next morning instead? This is a perfect example of both instinctive and adaptive thinking. Instinctive thinking is the kind of thinking we do with emotions and with our gut. Adaptive thinking is harder, even uncomfortable at times, and it takes time to employ empathy or do more research before you react. Adaptive thinking is the kind of thinking we need to do with social media, because our instincts are being tricked and we have to use critical thinking skills instead of being tricked into action.

We look for affirmation for what we believe is true, but mainly this can be overridden by our own confirmation bias. We find that everyone we agree with is saying it which gives it social proof. This reaffirms to us this content that aligns with our beliefs must be true. But we need to change our pattern recognition. We need to start seeing the intent and the marketing tactics being used. Check out *The Evolution of Thought: Why We Think the Way We Do* by Roger Bourke White Jr. for a more in-depth look at instinctive and adaptive thinking.

1.9 Curated Content is the New Free Market

Imagine you live in a neighborhood that has one small grocery store that carries the essentials. Imagine the only kind of jelly this store carries is grape jelly. No one complains and they sell plenty of grape jelly so they just keep stocking it. Now imagine you find yourself at a far away grocery store and there you see strawberry jelly. You buy it and you love it! You tell all your neighbors and let them try it and now your local grocery store has been inundated with requests to stock strawberry jelly. Now the nearby store sells both strawberry and grape jelly and the strawberry jelly is selling even better than grape. When you ask the grocery store owner why they didn't start selling strawberry before now he replies, "Nobody requested it and grape jelly was a top seller for us."

This story illustrates how online content appears to us in its simplest terms. Content you see online is curated in response to what it thinks you want to see based on what you have interacted with in the past. I want you to be aware that everything you see online is curated content. Curated content means you are being shown preselected content first and you have to do some real digging to see more. Online companies are using algorithms and artificial intelligence (AI) to show you what they think you want to see. This isn't a concept of the future, it isn't even a new concept, it has been happening for years and it is getting more and more targeted. This happens in your social media feeds, your Google searches, your Amazon orders, and even your Netflix account. Why do they do this? Because target markets are easier to get a response from then broad ones. Just like the grocery store example, there is no reason for them to change until their customer does. And as long as grape jelly is a top seller, they will keep selling the grape jelly.

This means you created the curation of information yourself and the Internet keeps reaffirming you. So none of us are starting from an objective place when searching for anything. We assume that the information surrounding us is a free market and we are seeing everything . . . but we aren't. We aren't even given the option upfront to be equally informed as someone with a different viewpoint. Our only options are what is on the shelf in front of us. We are given the option of information with our bias and more information featuring our bias. It is target marketing at a level that we are largely unaware of and it contributes to our understanding of the world.

A fun and slightly terrifying experiment to do is to Google the exact same words next to someone with opposing political views from you. The results will be drastically different. A great place to compare curated feeds of both conservative and liberal viewpoints side-by-side is Blue Feed, Red Feed created by the Wall Street Journal to see just how different they are. The predictive content we see everyday may make our lives more convenient, but the price we pay for being a target market is an actual change in how we perceive the world compared to someone else. We now see the world through a curated view that we didn't choose willingly and which most people are simply unaware of.

1.10 The Information Gap

So if all the content you are seeing is curated, think about how much information you aren't seeing? You're not even given the chance to make a truly objective decision because of the curation of the information. This actual gap in information creates huge misunderstandings and makes empathy almost impossible. Without even knowing it we are seeing narratives from 'our side' about the 'other side.' This makes information we receive about opposing viewpoints closer to assumptions than actual informed understanding.

I can't tell you how many lists I have seen posted online with titles like "Ten Things That Will Drive Liberals Nuts" and "The Biggest Conservative Lies" that are completely off base. They are one group writing about another group with a huge gap of information and therefore a complete lack of understanding. So instead of providing insight they are providing assumptions, and they just make you sound ignorant when you share them. If you want to know what liberals are thinking, read a liberal article, not a conservative one telling you what liberals are thinking and vice versa. The same advice goes for any demographic you are not a part of. If you don't personally know any Muslims, than you can read a book by a Muslim such as *I Am Malala: The Girl Who Stood Up for Education and Was Shot by the Taliban* by Malala Yousafzai, or go to an open house at a mosque instead of asking someone who isn't a Muslim or reading articles written by people who aren't Muslim.

1.11 Guilty Until Proven Innocent

Every single post you see online should be considered false until proven otherwise. This will be hard at first because if something aligns with our opinion we are far more likely to argue its validity than to accept any facts against it. This is considered a confirmation bias when we only see truth in information that aligns with our already held beliefs. But if you start to see online posts as marketing to elicit you to react, it doesn't matter what political opinion you have. Marketing tactics are used no matter what side you are on. This entire book is full of marketing examples to help you give everything you see a second thought.

You don't have to read this book all the way through cover to cover. Skip around, find items that are relevant to you, and take what you need. Anytime we are more knowledgeable about what we post and why we are posting we are being a better version of ourselves online.

CHAPTER 2

ONLINE ETIQUETTE

2.1 Why Do Online Arguments Escalate?

Our human tendency to stack things is a common theme many people in the self-help space touch on. Think of it this way—you wake up in the morning late, then you stub your toe, then you of course get toothpaste on your shirt, and before you know it your whole day is ruined and it just started! And from a marketing standpoint stacking makes a ton of sense too. We want what we promote to stack on beliefs you already have stacked up and we want you to stack on them even more. So we target you.

So think about how people argue on the Internet in the terms of stacking. If someone is posting something hateful, they are setting it up to be stacked upon with more hateful comments by others. If you look at content through the lens of 'How does this post want me to stack on to this?', it is easy to curb a reaction that will escalate an online argument. Think about it with hateful content put out there by elected officials, with rallies, with tweets, with memes, with the kind of language being used. That is all being done to make you stack on it with more hate. Don't fall for it.

2.2 Your Online Behaviors Are Influenced by Marketing Tactics

Marketers expertly understand online etiquette. Why? Because you buy what we are selling, figuratively and monetarily too. As a professional marketer I am the kind of person who knows how to analyze every word and turn a phrase. I also have the advantage of understanding the nuance of a #hashtag (using a # before a word is often used for searching and also as commentary), online and pop-culture trends, and I keep up to date with changes in algorithms and audience engagement shifts. The minute I write this sentence things will change, but I will continue to pay attention and learn with the changes because it is my job.

You don't need to know the things marketers do. But you do need to know basic online etiquette, because everything you say and post online is a type of marketing. You are marketing your beliefs, who you hate, and all sorts of ways you may not see. And there is power in discussion that isn't hateful. I can't tell you how many times people have opened my eyes to new information through a discussion online. But so many people end up in fights that they basically anticipate them. Many even make fun of anyone who makes an effort to try to have meaningful discussions online about politics. Don't be shamed into silence. Instead learn and do better. Megan Phelps-Roper gave an extraordinary TED Talk: *I grew up in the Westboro Baptist Church. Here's why I left.* She shares her personal story of the extraordinary power online conversations had on her life and how it helped her leave a cult.

2.2 This meme is one of many memes used to shame people online for discussing politics by claiming it is a waste of time.

I am not an expert at difficult conversations. In fact I tend to avoid them, however by leaning on what I know about online etiquette from a marketing lens I have virtually changed my experience online when discussing politics and I want to share with you that insight. But If you want to know more about how to effectively have great conversations, I suggest you read *Talking Across the Divide: How to Communicate with People You Disagree with and Maybe Even Change the World* by gay Christian activist and author Justin Lee. He really knows what he is talking about and has over twenty years of experience with this topic.

2.3 Are You Responsible For Other People's Feelings Online?

> **"When you hurt someone on the Internet, you hurt them in real life."**
>
> - Brett Culp

The basic answer to this is of course not if you had good intentions. And you can't always predict what will upset others because we all don't have the same life experiences. In your daily life you don't go around trying to be mean to people just for attention, yet tons of us do it online. And I firmly believe we all know exactly what kind of attention we are looking for most of the time when we post online. I can't count how many times I have seen the words "I am just going to leave this here," with a meme posted from a troll account where people are being mean on purpose to get attention and to start something.

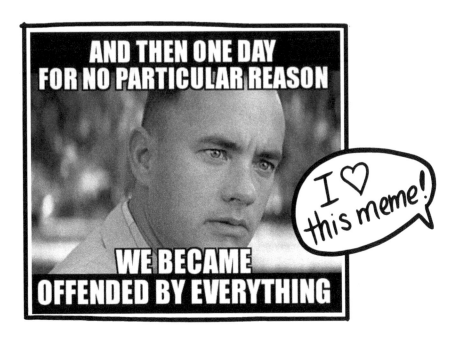

2.3 People know what kind of attention they are looking for when they post online. Pretending you shouldn't be blamed for negative reactions to what you post online is the same as not being responsible for what you say to someone. You are responsible even if you didn't think it was going to be offensive.

> **"It's insane to do something you know is insulting to another human being and expect no repercussions."**
>
> - Jack White

Freedom of speech doesn't mean freedom from consequences. It never has. If you say something publically you will probably have to face the consequences. Those consequences aren't going to jail but it doesn't mean none exist.

And I can tell you right now; people speaking out for a better world are also facing consequences. But there are way more people speaking out by posting hateful memes and they think no consequences await them. They do this mainly out of an emotional response to having their beliefs challenged and it satisfies them because it garners attention. It may be a mix of positive and negative attention but it's attention nonetheless. And a major consequence of those divisive posts is making the world a worse place. These posts also have consequences that can include lost friendships, harming people they care about, and in some cases, legal ramifications and lost jobs. So if you lose a friendship, strain a relationship, or even lose a job because of something you posted, you need to acknowledge that those are your consequences for your actions.

A good rule of thumb is: If you wouldn't put it on a sign in your yard for all to see, then don't say it on the Internet, because that is basically what you are doing. If you are afraid of the social repercussions of a sign in your front yard that all your neighbors can see, then why would you post something for everyone to see that can never truly be deleted? We will get more into this topic in the next section.

2.4 You Are Responsible for Everything You Ever Post Online

Your great-grandchildren and great-great-grandchildren will see everything you ever posted online and it will be your legacy. This might seem basic but I know so many people that write hateful e-mails, messages, and other posts they delete, believing they are secret hidden communication. They aren't. It only takes a second for someone to screengrab what you wrote before it is deleted, it only takes a second to take a photo of a screen before a snap disappears, and no one owes you anonymity for hateful words you write in private online. It is a cultural norm to share that content with identifying information blocked out, but no one owes you that.

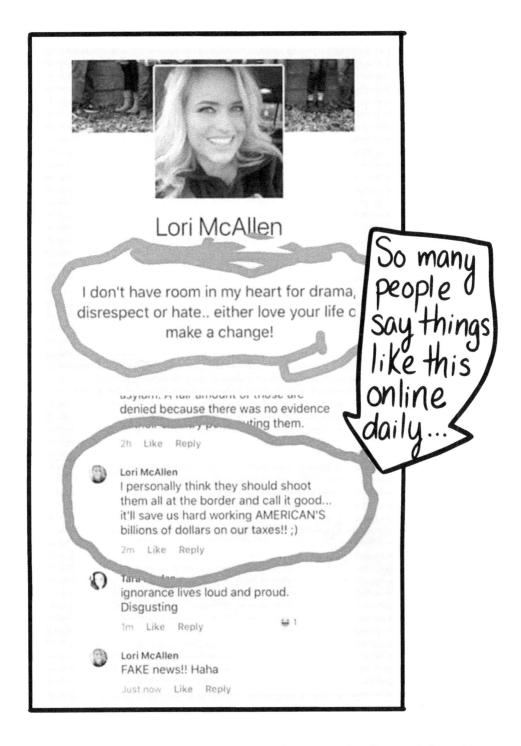

2.4 Someone screengrabbed what Lori McAllen posted online and shared it without doing her the added courtesy of obscuring out her name to make her statement anonymous. The post went viral and there are thousands of articles about her online featuring this post. It had repercussions with her employment and this one horrible statement will follow her the rest of her life.

We have all made stupid mistakes online saying things we shouldn't. We are all learning and hopefully we are making smarter decisions today than we did yesterday. We have witnessed what happens when old posts come out to haunt people. Politicians have had to step down and people have lost their jobs. But what I think is more important is to understand that when you are gone, your digital footprint won't be. Just as I am fascinated to go through my grandparents' personal letters they saved, my grandchildren will go through everything I wrote online to get to know who I was. And just as my grandmother probably never gave a second thought to her personal correspondences being read, our private conversation online could someday come to life. What will your online footprint say about you to the future generations?

2.5 Aggressive Language

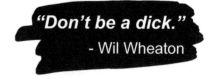

"Don't be a dick."
- Wil Wheaton

Hate and aggressive language is an attempt to feel significant. Hateful language is verbal abuse. Wrap your head around that. If you are being aggressive online you are being abusive to another person, all while trying to sound important, which means you are harming someone while trying to make them and others believe you are important. It also instantly markets to people who read your posts what group of people you hate and lets people know if you are against them.

"Calling someone ugly doesn't make you any prettier, and calling someone stupid doesn't make you any smarter."
- Tina Fey

Online we tend to be very unaware of our aggressive language. I have found we have to be actively conscious to avoid it because most people's posts are aggressive to begin with. They are created by trolls to be that way and the language they use prompts us to stack on more of the same unless we consciously choose to not follow suit.

Here are some big ones to watch out for:
- Name calling, including any kind of nickname. Calling someone stupid or saying Obummer, never Trumper, and tRUMP are all the same.

- Racist language such as Pocahontas (for Elizabeth Warren) or Obama bin Laden.

- Dehumanizing name-calling, such as 'pig' or 'creature.'

- Using name-calling that implies someone is a criminal like murderer, baby killer, or rapist.

- USING ALL CAPS WHICH READS AS ANGRY SCREAMING.

- Using contemptible language like 'lazy liberal' or 'ignorant republican.'

- Batching people negatively with phrasing like "typical liberal" or "just like a republican to assume."

- Swearing always reads as yelling.

- Threats, even if said in jest, such as the common phrase, "Go jump off a bridge."

- Telling someone to leave the country if they have a different belief than you.

We also have to be really careful with the use of loaded words and phrases. Mostly because they're disrespectful or in reference to actual historical events and people use them out of context to exaggerate someone's political affiliation or claim victimhood. They tend to escalate conversations just as any other form of aggressive language, but are great marketing tools. Some common ones are: witch hunt, race card, socialism, anchor babies, fake news, illegals, snowflake, Nazis, Hollywood elite, sharia law, baby killers, etc.

2.6 Your Bias Will Always Make it Look Like the Other Guy Treated You Worse

> "People will forget what you said, people will forget what you did, but people will never forget how you made them feel."
> - Maya Angelou

I know how words affect us from a marketing standpoint, and I know that when something is personal to us, it resonates with us more and we have far more empathy. Many people act as if words don't matter. But they would freak out if those words were directed at them. Words don't feel the same when they aren't directed at you.

So take a look at the sentences highlighted below about Jenny. You don't particularly like Jenny and she has never really been nice to you or done anything nice for anyone you know. Now read these following statements about her:

"Jenny can't even get to class on time and always looks like crap. She needs to try harder."

"Jenny shouldn't even go to this school if she can't at least try. Probably a charity case. Getting her expelled would do her and us all a favor from having to put up with her half-assed trying."

Not too bad, right? They aren't nice but they aren't terrible. Now imagine you know Jenny. Let's say she is your little cousin and her mother works two jobs. Jenny gets her two siblings fed and bathed at night and gets them to school in the morning while her mother works. Jenny barely has time to study, but she is a good kid and basically pulling the weight of an adult. She not only attends a private high school but she is also active in her church.

Now read those sentences again. How would it make you feel knowing all you know about Jenny? Now that I made Jenny important to you, does it hurt more? Do you now recognize the accusations in the sentences escalate in a way that you didn't perceive the first time? It went from criticizing, to name calling, to an outright threat on her, and that is terrifying. But if you don't care about Jenny, it just isn't personal to you.

How does this make you rethink things you have said online or have heard others say?

2.7 Parroting

Most of what we post online is just parroted information. We are just reposting something someone else created or taking phrases from another post we saw. We all do it. Parroting is marketing in action, and here's why:

If you asked a 100 people from the same political party to say in their own words what they think about a political topic, you would get about a 100 different answers with all kinds of nuance and even some uncertainty.

Now give those people a single meme that is from their political side, and they all will share it as if they came up with that answer on their own. And as people like it and comment on it, they get notifications to go back and reread it and cement it as their opinion. They will even defend this post viciously as if it is sacred scripture, completely internalizing that this is their opinion.

2.7 When hundreds of people align with a single statement you are shifting public opinion. Now think about the thousands of memes with some being shared by millions of people proclaiming that this meme is their opinion.

But it isn't their actual opinion. It is a stranger's opinion. For all we know, the stranger is probably a troll at best or an extremist lying at worst. Think about it. This might be the most obvious but overlooked idea in the book. When we repost something, it isn't actually our opinion. We just agreed with it or think it is witty, and feel it will really stick it to those 'other people.' We followed the post's logic according to our confirmation bias. It is actually creepy if you think about spreading memes as if they were real conversation:

"I like this meme. I am going to share it as my opinion."

"I like this meme too! I am also going to share it as my exact opinion."

"I have no idea who made this, but this meme is obviously my opinion too!"

"Mine too!"

"Mine too!"

"Oh this meme from a troll account speaks for me."

"I will defend this stranger's pointed meme against all who criticize!"

"How dare you criticize a divisive post created by a stranger! This stranger's post proves you unequivocally wrong!"

"Oh this meme truly speaks for us all."

"Who else thinks this meme is exactly their opinion? I will share it to find out!"

"OMG Yessss! Tons of people I know think this meme is gospel!"

This creates absolute hive mind. No one agrees exactly like this, but one after another we have all fallen in line in exact agreement because of something made by a stranger (who could be a total creeper). We have internalized it as our own. And it is absolutely making our country more divided, because it means strangers and troll accounts with purposefully divisive content are speaking and thinking for us. And this is narrowing what should be a diverse opinion pool.

Remember, everything that is put online is meant to be shared, so by sharing and reposting, we are doing exactly what that post was marketed to do. We are being a complicit consumer by spreading that content. We have helped a troll get more attention. We fulfilled their need for attention with the exact response they hoped for. We have fed their (most likely nutso) agenda and have decided to take up their stance, defend it, and proclaim it as our own. Behold the power of marketing.

I am always blown away when people parrot memes and their concepts in real life as an original thought. It happens daily, especially coming from those who try to avoid politics online. You can attempt to ignore politics, but you truly can't, because memes are quick and you will see them. And it goes all the way up to the top. Our politicians, the current administration, and biased and far leaning news sources parrot this crap too. These ideas stick and are easy to internalize and regurgitate. Great marketing.

2.8 Flailing

Have you ever gotten into an online argument about an issue and the other person completely ignores what you are saying and keeps piling on a million unrelated points? They are flailing for any possible example they can grab onto so they can be right. Think about it as they can't bear to look at the evidence against their side or even acknowledge it, so they are pointing you and themselves everywhere else to ease their own mind. No one likes to be wrong, and we all want to be the good guy in every situation. If we are flailing, it is because we can't resolve what someone said (while still being right), so we are throwing everything we can at it. At this point in an online conversation, they aren't listening at all. Jonathan Haidt goes into great detail about this practice of flailing and other tactics we use to try to convince ourselves we are right in his book, *The Righteous Mind: Why Good People Are Divided by Politics and Religion.*

The best thing I have found we can do is acknowledge what they are saying. They aren't giving us the same courtesy, but if we show that we hear them, we can help de-escalate the conversation. We can also repeat what we said prior and ask them to acknowledge that statement. The best way I have found to bring a hysterical keyboard warrior back from flailing is listening, acknowledging, and pointing out how we aren't all that different. I also find guiding them back to our original point to be helpful. This sets a precedent and helps them to follow our lead to create a far more beneficial conversation. Will it always work? No, some people will flail so much that they can never be brought back to shore. We just have to let them sink and know we tried.

2.9 Nitpicking

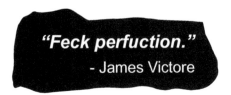

"Feck perfuction."
- James Victore

This goes hand in hand with flailing. We have all experienced someone picking every tiny little thing we say apart. Sometimes it looks like correcting our grammar or it can be dumping a ton of tangential facts and using as much exact terminology as possible to try to prove someone wrong. Their response is usually extremely long winded. They are trying to sound important and smart. But all they sound like is a giant callous know it all.

Just recently a friend of mine was out protesting to stop gun violence, and one of his friends online posted a giant argument against him, asking for his definition of mass shootings, rambling off caliber differences, and picking apart another commenter's usage of the word automatic. This person wrote over 350 words nitpicking about exact specifications of firearms and technical definitions of mass shootings and instead of sounding smart, he sounded like he cared more about being right than actual lives lost.

I am not saying facts aren't important, and I firmly believe we should correct people when they are spreading misinformation, but nitpicking has nothing to do with the facts. It is a type of flailing where we are grabbing onto perceived missteps or anything possible to try to sound smart, trying to justify our opinion, and trying to humiliate another person. My friend was out protesting because a loved one used a gun to commit suicide, and he had previously lived in Orlando where the PULSE shooting happened. He was protesting for our lawmakers to make change, when the nitpicker chimed in. If you compare this to a non political issue, it is like someone protesting people dying in car accidents and standing up asking for changes to be made to the automobile industry and someone gives them a list of parts in the engine as a reason to stop requesting change. You would never do that.

Here's an idea—if you spend time nitpicking politicians, you just look petty to their supporters and they think you don't focus on real issues. Think about that for a second— how many politicians do you think make missteps just in hopes you nitpick them so *you* look bad?

2.9 J. K. Rowling is notorious for nitpicking Trump's bad grammar. In one of his tweets he used pour instead of the correct word pore and after he posted a corrected tweet she taunted him about the grammar mistake.

2.10 Batching/Tropes Don't Help Anything

We might not know what these are, but you can think of them as a stereotype. They are generalities that usually have a negative connotation. I am going to go into them more in-depth when talking about memes and marketing tactics, but a great way to identify many of them is if they have the word 'all' (or some other term batching people together) somewhere in the concept. For example:

"All Americans should speak English if they want to live here!"

"Liberals want to take all our guns!"

"All protesters are paid."

"All conservatives are bigots."

"Millennials are all addicted to their phones and are all lazy."

"Women who are pro-choice are all pro-abortion."

"Traditional gender roles are how God made us."

"Women need to act more like ladies and less like men to keep their uniqueness."

"Drug addicts all deserve what they get."

"Why would I want to go to a church full of child molesters?"

"Poor people just need to pull themselves up by their bootstraps."

"All men are in real danger now because all sexual encounters can be called rape."

Basic batching memes and tropes are everywhere and there is another extremely common but more complex form of batching to be aware of. This kind of post is assuming a stance on a political topic based on another assumed political stance. Think about this technique as ideas presented in this format: all Liberals believe this one thing so they all must believe this other thing too. It is an extreme over simplification and batches people in multiple tropes together.

All these phrases and ideologies are oversimplifications of real issues and they batch people into a lump of assumptions. Yet the content we post online doubles down on these ideas. We become the marketers and perpetrators of piss poor ideas. We put up these black and white stances and they are all basic tropes that we only believe to be true when they meet our bias. It is easy to spot a trope when you know it isn't true, but if it has become an anecdotal truth in your community it will be much harder to see.

2.11 Partisan Integrity

"Everybody believes in accountability until it's their guy. Accountability is meaningless unless it's for everybody — whether it's the leader of a network, or the leader of the free world."

\- Stephen Colbert

An overarching theme that has caused so many of us to lose faith in people is the lack of integrity when it comes to partisan accountability. We know so many people who are not holding their allies to the same standards they hold their enemies to. And in all honesty I don't think it is easy to see when we ourselves are doing it. It takes real self-reflection to hold those we support to our own standards of accountability and not yield based on who they are. We make up justifications how 'this time it is different,' but in reality we are following justifications where we want them to go.

Honestly this feels like cult mentality sometimes when people so blatantly change opinion based on 'their team.' But I can clearly see how the marketing tactics used to ingrain ideas have changed how people think. Most of us can't even be reasoned with and facts don't seem to matter. This has completely changed people I know, love, and trust, and I find it terrifying. I can't make excuses for their actions, but I can offer my own insights that have helped me self-reflect on how I hold others and myself accountable.

Anytime I question an action or find myself wanting to vilify/judge something or someone, I try to ask myself if it would be the same reaction if the tables were turned? I try to make lateral comparisons. For one, I originally was inclined to think poorly of Melania Trump because of her relationship history and career choices with soft-core porn. But then I remembered my own rule. I do not judge women on how they use their bodies or in a way I wouldn't judge a man. This applies to a stripper, a news anchor, a teenager, a rape victim, a prostitute, Hilary Clinton, and certainly Melania. I also don't hold her accountable for her husband's sexual indiscretions. And if that applies to her, that applies to Hillary Clinton and any other woman who has been cheated on. Even though she is part of an administration I almost never agree with, I hold myself to my own standard. I don't waiver in my integrity when it is convenient to me to pick out someone as an easy target.

By asking myself if the behavior is justified when the tables are turned, I have been able to call myself out on my own tendencies that lack integrity. Am I perfect? No. But it has helped me see if I've been biased in how I've handled situations.

2.11 Sometimes memes point out the blatant lack of partisan integrity. The Trump administration has been dogged on criticizing the nepotism surrounding Hunter Biden yet Trump has given the leadership of his empire to his children and even given them positions in the government with unprecedented levels of clearance simply because they are his children.

2.12 My Social Media Rules

> *"Sure the goal is important. But never forget that each individual instance matters, too—each is a snapshot of the whole. The whole isn't certain, only the instances are.*
>
> *How you do anything is how you can do everything. We can always act right."*
>
> -Ryan Holiday,
>
> *The Obstacle is the Way: The Ancient Art of Turning Adversity to Advantage*

I know having social media 'rules' seems extreme, but if we have no standard, how will we hold ourselves accountable? That is why I consciously have rules to help me do better. And do I always follow my rules? Heck no! I am not perfect, but I am trying to be a better version of myself everyday. My integrity is defined by everything I do and I take responsibility for that. I refuse to sink to certain levels I see people sink to, so I have defined what that means to me.

How did I come up with these rules? I used lateral thinking and comparison and my own inner compass to guide me. Sometimes I would see things that really got to me and I had to think about them differently to figure out if I would accept that behavior if it was directed towards others. My conclusion usually was that if it hurt me, it must hurt others, and these rules have helped me hold my allies to the same standards that I hold my adversaries and myself. Just because it is 'my team' doesn't mean I can lower my personal integrity.

Not all these rules are strictly political but it is surprising how they have helped me in political conversations. I hope these will give you some ideas of how you can post with more grace and more responsibility.

Here are my current rules (they are always changing as needed):

My **Social Media** Rules

1. I am supportive, caring, and kind online.
2. I fact-check everything I share.
3. No one speaks for me. I own every word.
4. I don't use aggressive language/imagery.
5. I don't share voyeuristic posts.
6. I watch myself for discriminatory bias.
7. I don't change others' protest language.
8. I don't victim shame.
9. I don't share hurt/dead animals or people.
10. I unfriend/unfollow for hate speech, death threats, racism, victim shaming, and EXCESSIVE cursing.

2.11.1 What would be on your list of social media rules?

I am supportive, caring, and kind online.

Every time I am on social media I will be social. I always try to be supportive to others and comment on at least one person's post. It is called social media for a reason. Many people lurk and say nothing as a tactic to avoid conflict and keep their feed from being impacted by the algorithm, but being silent isn't helping make social media a place we want it to be. By not participating you are helping the status quo maintain as it is. I try to show up as my best self and my best self is supportive, caring, and kind. Does it mean I can't be critical, share my opinion, or stand up for others and my beliefs? No, absolutely not. Showing up as my best self does not mean I have to show up as a doormat. Does it mean I always succeed? No. But I am always trying to do better.

I fact check everything I share.

Yes, I have been fooled multiple times and have shared things I thought were true that weren't. What matters is I am always trying to do better. When I see memes without links, articles from sites I have never heard of, or superlative language, it alerts my inner marketer immediately to verify the information. There really is no excuse not to. My phone is within reach at all times, and just because I believe something to be real doesn't mean that it is. In a time where the entire world's knowledge is at the tip of our fingers, being ignorant is a choice, and I chose to be responsible for what I post. I owe that to myself and those who know me.

As you go through this book you will learn all kinds of things to look out for to fact-check posts. And just the thought of 'could this possibly be untrue or false logic?' will stop you from posting 99% of the things you think you need to post.

No one speaks for me. I own every word.

When you repost something, you are basically just regurgitating someone else's thoughts. And when we parrot what someone else says, I find we begin to internalize the idea as if it was our own, when it truly wasn't an original thought at all. Following someone else's logic to where they want me to go is not how I want to communicate or understand the world. It is lazy, and parroting/sharing divisive ideas isn't helpful. If I have something to say I will speak for myself.

Also, I own every word I ever put out into the digital space. All of them. I am accountable for what I say in private messages too. No one owes me anonymity if I said something hateful, hurtful, or wrong in the past even if I didn't know better at the time. I own every word in every shared meme, every moment in a shared video, and every word in every shared article.

I don't use aggressive language or images

I don't use name calling, bullying insults, all caps yelling, excessive swearing, or other forms of aggressive language, because it always escalates conversations. And I don't share articles or memes that have it either. Why? Because I own everything I post and I refuse to sink that low.

I never threaten anyone or tell them to harm themselves. I can't tell you how many times I have seen people do this. And many times it is in a passive aggressive context or using a saying such as 'go jump off a bridge,' but it is still really uncalled for.

I also never tell anyone they should leave the country. I have been told multiple times online that I should leave the country by people I personally know (mainly when I stood up for children by taking part in the March for Our Lives). I was marching to hold our country accountable for children's safety and I had actual parents I knew personally tell me I was unAmerican for wanting that (I don't have children but I will always stand up for their safety.)

I also don't use swearing because it is a form of verbal assault and not everyone is comfortable with swearing. So if I do post something with swearing in it I usually include the NSFW (Not Safe for Work) acronym to let people know there will be swearing. I share lots of motivational content by Gary Vaynerchuck and he drops the f-bomb all the time. I don't want to affront anyone who wasn't expecting that kind of language.

> "Do the best you can until you know better. Then when you know better, do better."
>
> - Maya Angelou

I never use racist terms or hate speech and try to be politically correct, and when I know better, I do better, because it is common courtesy and this backlash against being politically correct is really about people being ashamed of getting it wrong. They are afraid they don't know what to say, so they just say the wrong thing and then go on diatribes about 'free speech' and how being 'politically correct' has gone too far. But in reality they don't want to look stupid and are deflecting when they don't know what is appropriate. The trend of taking pride in not saying what is respectful is basically taking a stance of ignorance and taking of stance against even trying.

One really good example I heard in regards to being politically correct has to do with nicknames. I go by my full name Katherine and by lots of nicknames: Katie, Kate, and Kat, but I don't like to be called Kathy. Some people have called me Kathy and I have corrected them asking them not to call me that. Now imagine if they kept doing it anyway because they liked Kathy and didn't care what I wanted to be called? That is pretty disrespectful, right? It isn't up to them to determine what I should be called—it is up to me. That is the same as being politically correct, but the stakes are usually much higher. Once you know better, do better. It is the respectful thing to do.

I also don't share intimidating images—things like someone holding a giant rifle saying, "Try to come at my guns" is a perfect example. But there are other examples such as images of ICE officers saying, "We will get you out of our country" or photos of people wearing racist attire. They are all implying physical threats.

I don't share voyeuristic posts

I don't share voyeuristic posts. What does that mean? If I didn't get permission from a private citizen (not including public figures) to share their image around the Internet for my own enjoyment, I don't share them. This includes funny memes featuring people making funny faces or being caught in awkward positions. We have all seen these and laughed at them. Many times images of private citizens are photographed out in public and are shared to shame their weight or behavior, but they were unaware their photo was taken. Don't get me wrong, I used to share these all the time, but now I know better.

Any post where a private citizen is being shamed for behavior that isn't hurting anyone shouldn't be shared. It is the same thing as a schoolyard bully making fun of a kid for how they dress or their haircut. It is the exact same thing only worse. Now they are permanently viral across the Internet without their consent and that is a total violation of their privacy and consent. And If you shared the image you are responsible for it.

*2.11.2 These women were shamed at a baseball game by the announcer and
then were shared around the internet as a token image of how this generation
can't go anywhere without being on their phones and therefore miss actual
events they attend. But what is worse about this image is you can clearly see a
prompt to tweet an image of yourself right on this image. These women were
probably following the prompt they were given and then shamed for it. Of all
the people who shared this viral content making fun of these women I didn't see
one person even realize the prompt to tweet yourself was on the image right
in front of them. Proving we only see what marketing tells us we are seeing,
because it is funnier to shame these women than to use critical thinking of what
is actually shown in the image.*

Is it against the law? No. But if I share a private citizen's photo across the Internet,
it better be from a news story where they were aware their photo was being taken
and the context of them being shared has to be in the same context they thought
the photo was for. I don't feel I have the right to put my weird political opinion on
a stranger and share them across the Internet. Did I always know this? No. But
now I do. How would you feel if millions of people spread your image around with
a political opinion you disagreed with? Or what if you became Internet famous
because people made fun of you?

I also don't share memes that feature little kids. Do you know how many memes
I see daily featuring someone's kid being passed around the Internet with some
random saying on their image? Think about it—you didn't get permission from
the parents to share that, you have no idea if their beliefs even align with what
is being said, and that child is too young to give consent and understand the
consequences of their image forever on the Internet out of their control. I don't
care if the parents made the meme. Odds are we will never know if they did and
the child is too young to give consent regardless.

I watch myself for discriminatory bias

I am learning everyday just like everyone else. I try to not post discriminatory tropes based on gender, sexual orientation, religion, race, place of birth, income, and other groupings we tend to batch people into. For me I use lateral thinking as discussed earlier in this chapter. It helps me call myself out on my own bullshit excuse of "This situation is different because…"

> **"If it's not true for all of us, it shouldn't be true for any of us."**
> - Rachel Hollis

Where this shows up the most in my life has been in the way I talk about women. I constantly have to compare how I talk about women and men and this is the area in which I have had the most personal growth. I don't post judgment on a woman based on how she is dressed, if she is likeable, how she lives her life, her choices for her family, her sexual conduct, her physical appearance, what she does with her body, or the sexual conduct of her significant other. We constantly do this to women and we never do it to men. We always hold women to a double standard men don't face and it needs to stop. If I am not judging a man for something, then I need not judge a woman.

I don't change others' protest language

> **"Respect costs nothing, means everything."**
> - Taylor Cisco

I don't change others' protest language unless it is mine to change, because I have no right to tell someone what they 'really meant to say' or how they 'really should protest' for my own personal comfort. It is just that simple. Changing someone's protest language is taking something that isn't yours to begin with. And what you are doing is basically name calling and mocking. That is it.

If you think of the nonpolitical example I shared earlier it really helps. I don't like it when people call me Kathy. I like Katherine, so don't call me Kathy. Some people are assholes and call me Kathy anyways. Yeah, that is mean and disrespectful of my wishes. Now imagine if people were protesting a wrongful death and you changed the name of their movement. That is a line of respect I won't cross.

I don't victim shame

I never victim shame. Unless I was in the room where the incident happened, I have no idea what that victim has been through. Say I victim shamed someone and I am wrong? What kind of monster would that make me? And the scary part is many of us become monsters if the accused is on our team. Our confirmation bias makes us believe that we know our side better and we victim shame like it is our job. Many even take it further and harass the victims and make claims of how the accused are really the victims. Our country embraces the system of innocent until proven guilty, which means victims not only have to go through something horrible, but then have to prove beyond a reasonable doubt it happened, relive it over and over again, and justice is not guaranteed. Just look at the thousands of untested rape kits in this country and the single digit percentage conviction rates for reported rape cases and you can see how the uphill battle is not only emotional but systemic in our country.

I have been subpoenaed once to testify as a witness at a grand jury hearing and it was traumatic. I wasn't the victim, I was just a witness. My former-self jeered at Law & Order victims about being cowards in the face of injustice, not wanting to testify. I realized real quick what it must be like being a victim and having to relive the worst day of your life and confront someone who may never even be brought to justice. That one night was the most traumatic event in my life and I just wished it never happened. I can't imagine how a victim would feel. Seriously, I can't imagine. I refuse to possibly add to what someone is going through. I owe them at least as much grace as the accused, no matter whose side I am on.

I don't share hurt/dead animals or people

I don't share these images because unless someone asked to see them, I don't believe I have the right to make them appear in their feed. Everyone's thresholds are different and I try to respect that.

I grew up in hunting country and farm country, so dead animals were recreation and people's livelihoods. But seeing an animal that was gunned down for sport has always gutted me. Now imagine people who didn't grow up surrounded with this culture? What must that be like for them? Even if I am spreading awareness of a tragedy, I refuse to cross my threshold.

When it comes to hurt humans, many people post pictures of wounds and such but again you don't know if people will be squeamish looking at these. Also, there is a trend to post videos of people's last moments just before they die. This is usually to draw attention to the tragedy and people do it out of outrage or sympathy. But I can't think of any worse way of disrespecting the dead. If I die in a tragedy, I sure as hell wouldn't give anyone permission to spread my demise around the Internet, and I refuse to do that to someone who obviously can't be asked for their permission. And just think about the families—people loved this person, and they probably don't want to be scrolling through the Internet and just stumble upon watching them die no matter how outraged you are or whatever justice you are calling for when sharing it.

I unfriend/unfollow for hate speech, death threats, racism, victim shaming, and excessive cursing

I can't believe I have to talk about these but here we go. I truly believe we all need to examine what we tolerate from those in our life even if it is online.

> *"You are always in control of two things, what you give and what you accept."*
>
> - Trent Shelton

I will not tolerate hate speech.

I will not tolerate death threats. I had to unfriend at least a dozen people I grew up with after the Parkland shooting because they posted about how they wanted to take their guns and shoot those kids and people who took part in the March for Our Lives. Just horrible. Caring people are protesting children being killed in school and people I knew posted how they wanted to kill them for it. I don't care if they were mad or just kidding.

I will not tolerate racism. I understand we all have a learning curve. And I even screw up not realizing something I have grown up saying is actually racist. But intentional racism is a solid HELL NO.

If you want to know how I feel about victim shaming, see rule #8.

Excessive swearing may seem weird to people, but when you swear online you are yelling. I have enough stress in my life without having to see people yelling online about everything. There are better ways to communicate.

CHAPTER 3

HOW TO SEE MARKETING TACTICS

3.1 Your Brain Doesn't Work How You Think It Does

> *"People need to be reminded more often than they need to be instructed."*
>
> - Samuel Johnson.

We are all influenced by marketing, even unintentional marketing. Blame your brain. They say that 80% of your daily thoughts are the same thoughts repeating themselves. As a marketer I can see this, considering how repetitive our daily lives are. We were taught consistently to have the beliefs we have, we see the same people everyday, do the same routines, we even consume the same media daily. You are reminded that your opinion of the world is right just by your daily experience. Without you ever knowing it, marketing takes advantage of this.

A famous example of unintentional marketing comes from Mars candy bars. They use marketing to sell their product and test different types of marketing to boost sales. At one point Mars bars started to track an increase in sales that didn't align with any marketing. So what caused it? The Mars Rover landing caused it. The Mars Rover was on the news constantly after the landing. It was not because people were buying Mars bars to celebrate. It was completely unconscious. The name Mars was being put in front of people over and over, day after day, and this was free marketing for the company![3.1.1] What beliefs are the people around you marketing to you daily that you don't even realize?

Marketing at its best is done for how our brain really works not for how we think our brain works. All marketers test strategies and double-down on what works. If they use a tactic or even a phrase and they get the response they want, they will do it over and over again. The online marketing of media, trolls, and politics consistently leans in on that idea. All of it is just repeating what works. Once you know marketing tricks you can't look at a meme or an article or even someone's behavior without seeing the tactics. Once you see these tactics it is extremely frustrating to watch people fall for them again and again. Let's amp up our critical thinking skills and take a look at classic marketing techniques used online.

3.2 Marketing Calendars, Strategies, and Teams

Despite our brains not working as we thing they do, it is good to keep in mind that marketing is planned. Public figures of any kind have agencies, writers, publicists, and social media specialists backing them up. There are entire teams doing polling of which words get the best reactions and should be used again. The entire year, if not many years in advance, are planned to make sure messages are pushed when needed.

Everything is so intricately planned that you have been part of the testing without even knowing it—if you interacted with content (or not), that has helped marketers plan exactly what to do next and how to phrase it. Even timing, such as early morning fiascos, purposefully take full advantage of morning, afternoon, and evening news cycles. Just because words may sound plainly spoken and off the cuff, don't be fooled—a professional with 15+ years experience probably still wrote it to hit the right target market, at the right time of year, according to his or her team's research.

3.3 Faulty Logic and Misconceptions

The number one marketing tool is our behavior. We believe faulty logic without using critical thinking skills and we all have misconceptions about what is being posted online. Faulty logic and misconceptions fueled by some well-placed marketing tactics are a recipe for virality. That is why fake news spreads so quickly. We click share on impulse, never questioning the faulty logic or the truth behind what we share.

And faulty logic and misconceptions are guided by the following common marketing tactics. Being able to identify these will help us realize when someone is trying to sway our opinion in a certain direction.

3.4 Repetition Makes the Heart Grow Fonder

Any news is good news. There is a reason this phrase exists. Celebrities, public figures, and marketers all know that the human mind construes familiarity with fondness. It is just how our brains work. Think about how people feel devastated when a celebrity they adore lands in a scandal. They have watched that person on TV and in movies over and over and feel an affinity towards them even though they have never met them.

Radio stations take advantage of this too. When they try to make a song a hit, they will smoosh it between two big hit songs and play it over and over, day after day. Pretty soon we are requesting that new song because we have heard it so much we now love it. They are tricking us into loving it.

When you hear politicians talk, notice how many of them will repeat sentences or phrases. That is marketing. By repeating the message over and over, it gets solidly implanted in your head.

3.5 Timing

Timing is a big picture concept, but basically it is the easiest marketing tactic to plan. Marketing and communications teams know when certain big events are coming, so they plan accordingly on when to act. It is no coincidence that the US-Mexico border wall became an emergency as the House flipped to Democratic control. The GOP knew it was the number one issue Democrats were against, so they decided to push it at that time to make the Democrats look anti-American and rally the Republican base. It could have gone through any time before with a GOP controlled House, Senate, and White House. The timing was intentional. What tactics have you witnessed being perfectly timed?

3.6 Misdirection or Distraction

Misdirection or distraction is a technique that makes us look where they want us to. Many times it is name calling, an outrageous tweet, or some other kind of political stunt that gets all the media attention. These distraction stunts are worth millions in free advertising and are usually done intentionally. Don't be fooled by the off the cuff feeling. Many times online arguments and scandals are actually preplanned marketing.

Misdirection can also be utilized by taking advantage of the lack of attention. When the entire country is busy celebrating a holiday season or almost everyone is asleep late at night, these are great times to pass bills or make political maneuvers right under our noses with no one looking.

3.7 Sense of Urgency

Watch for how a sense of urgency is marketed to you around issues. This tactic goes hand in hand with Timing, Misdirection, and Distraction, and can use all those tools to aid in creating the urgency. It is used to get you to take action, and is a tactic leveraged in fundraising. If you see something that makes you think that you have to act right now but there isn't an actual timeline besides an artificial one created for you, then you have been hit by 'sense of urgency' marketing.These phrases can look something like: "DEADLINE TONIGHT!" "The next hudred donors are true patriots!" "April's dealine is almost here!"

3.8 The Triple Play

My favorite marketing tactic that leans on repetition and distraction is something I call 'The Triple Play.' It is a tactic that used to only be used by reality tv celebrities, but now the political world uses this tactic all the time. Here's how it works:

1. Say something horrible and get a huge viral controversy started with people on both sides sharing and talking about it. The more people talk and argue, the more viral it goes.

2. This now gets a ton of press because of the controversy, and the attention on what happened starts all over again in the media.

3. The offenders are now asked about the statement or action by the media and either apologize or double down on their original statement. Their answer goes viral, and again people start arguing about what originally happened. This has given one action the maximum amount of traction and consistent news presence possible.

And this tactic is completely predictable. They get three rounds of marketing off of one outlandish statement or action. They have just won the Internet. They get repetition of coverage they can use as a distraction and they time it accordingly. The Trump administration puts loaded statements in every rally and in every press conference just to create this cycle of constant media coverage. And why not? It is billions of dollars in free advertising being leveraged with well-planned statements or actions.

The offenders of 'The Triple Play' typically will blame the media for covering the controversies instead of more important news—controversies they intentionally created. These tricks are old and predictable but they really do work. Think about past celebrities that contantly stayed in the news for scandals. Hollywood has mastered this technique and now it has been leveraged by politics.

3.9 Faking Authenticity and Personal Attention

People absolutely love when political figures or celebrities are authentic. These people have years of experience in the public eye, they know how to get attention and how to keep it in a way we perceive as authentic. Nothing is as spontaneous as it seems because of the years of experience public figures have to draw on and the teams they have backing them up. What most people don't consider is how these people have communications and marketing teams and strategists telling them exactly what to talk about, what words work best, and even writing and posting the content in the voice of the person. Don't for a second think a celebrity or a politician doesn't have a whole team helping them, or years of experience to create the appearance of authenticity.

We are also completely fooled by personal attention on social media from public figures. One retweet, one liked post, one response, or one photo we took was shared and we now feel a personal connection to this public figure. It makes us feel significant and that is a longing all humans have. Engaging with fans is part of every single social media marketing strategy. They are as planned as any other marketing tactic, and they have secured you as a fan for life now. You might even take a screen grab of the interaction and share it with your friends. You have now become an advocate for them and given them more free marketing.

3.10 The Power of Nostalgia

People hate change and we often look back on our lives with rose colored glasses longing for better days and simpler times. But change is the only constant you can count on. It is perfectly fine to miss the old days but we tend to romanticize them because that makes us feel comforted. Which is why it is such a powerful marketing tool. I mean how many times have you watched your favorite movie or tv show? Also, we often don't think about is how it wasn't better times for everyone. Nastalgic romanticism can also be seen as a white privilege according to Robin DiAngelo in her book *White Fragility: Why It's So Hard for White People to Talk About Racism.*

Nostalgia is a hugely popular promise in political campaigning, especially towards conservatives and older Americans. 'Make America Great Again' anybody? It is often used in conjunction with promises to bring back outdated jobs or traditions. Whenever I hear someone promising to turn back the clock and make things the way they were, I always cringe, because intentionally not moving forward only means the world moves forward without you. And when you eventually have no choice but to change, it makes the change even more jarring. The concept seems comforting (which is why it is so popular), but really it sets you up for failure because the world is changing whether you accept it or not. And anyone who is selling you on the past is selling you on the markting tactic of nostalgia.

I had the pleasure of hearing Stephanie Coontz, the Director of Research and Public Education for the Council on Contemporary Families and advisor to MTV for its anti-bias campaign, speak about the *Dangers of Nostalgizing* and it was a real eye opener for me on the marketing dangers leveraging nostalgia. Her talk made me far more aware of how the comfort can blind us to intent.

3.11 Tradition, Patriotism, Respect, & Honor

All these qualities are important societal pillars. And I love traditions. But tradition, patriotism, respect, and honor are all subjective acts. Your family might not have the same tradition as others. Some famlies go to church, some celebrate May Day, some do historical reenactments, and some families do none of these traditions. Also one person's act of patriotism looks like another's act of disrespect. An act that is seen as honorable to some may be seen as dishonorable to others. Men taking a knee in protest for black men being killed are labeled disrespectful to our soldiers, yet some of those soldiers find their act of protest very patriotic. While some think waiving guns protesting opening up our economy from pandemic closures is a patriotic duty others see them as domestic terrorists. All of these attributes are just one side of a coin based on your subjective perspective.

That is why you should always be skeptical when they are waved in front of you to create hostility or hatred towards others. These attributes are often leveraged in tribalistic ways in politics. Tradition, patriotism, respect, and honor can be leveraged to maintain a harmful status quo and to shame those who dare to speak up against a harmful cultural norm. It is a type of marketing like anything else.

3.12 Shame, Guilt, and Blame

Often when partisan groups don't approve of the behavior of political adversaries and feel offended, they leverage shame, guilt, or blame to direct the wrath of their followers. These feelings are extremely powerful and primal and pull on our emotions, not logic. They are also subjective. The emotional response to these marketing tactics is so powerful that they tend to elicit some kind of response from people, and it's usually not putting our best foot forward. This book is full of memes using these tactics. When you see a meme ask yourself if they are shaming, blaming, or placing guilt on a group of people in it.

Whenever I see public figures leveraging these emotions I try to remember that my gut will respond strongly before my mind does. And I usually have to calm down before I can think clearly about these marketing tactics and the goal they are being used to attain. In the moment my emotions flare up, my instant reaction is not my best self.

3.13 Hate is Free Advertising

It costs about $50 in paid advertising to reach about 6,000 people on Facebook, yet hateful memes spread by the tens of thousands in minutes. Hate is absolutely unifying and energizing and a form of free marketing. It is painful to even say that, but it is the truth. Hating the same group of people can be extremely unifying. The tactic is used in wartime propaganda; we love to hate certain sports teams; and nothing is more satisfying than talking with our friends about something/ someone we all mutually hate.

The easiest way to unite people is to make them hate others. Hate has direct access to your instinctive thinking. It makes large groups easier to control by turning them into smaller target markets and pitting them against one another. Whenever I hear hatred being marketed to me, I know that I am being pandered to. This realization has stopped me from following crowd mentality more times than I can count.

But the force that spreads hate online is the arguing it creates. There are many people who will call out hate for what it is. The impassioned arguments of both sides spread the content like wildfire. This double engagement with posts created by arguments spreads the hate wider and wider on social media. If one person cheers on the hatred and their friend calls them out on it, there could be an argument lasting 15+, 30+, 100+ comments. This engagement tells social platforms that the content is popular and algorithms spread it faster and show it to more people.

3.14 Pandering to Fear

I truly believe a lot of people react and make political decisions out of fear. You see it in the way they talk online. They start name calling and they are irrational and inconsolable based on their fear. Unfortunately, pandering to that fear is a huge marketing tactic.

It works because it isn't logical, it is emotional. Yet people will try to put 'facts' together to justify their fear all the time. Even if they understand the feeling isn't exactly logical, they will look for anything to support the irrational fear. Fear is visceral and it generates stubbornness against looking for understanding, because the situation is now felt as life and death.

3.15 Bullying Tactics

> *"All of us have seen something like this. And we all had a role in it. Either we were bullies, or we were victims, or we saw bullying and didn't stop it."*
>
> - Melinda Gates
> *The Moment of Lift*

The easiest way to tell if someone doesn't have a justifiable argument is if they use bullying tactics. Most of these tactics fall under aggressive language. Name calling, insults, swearing, innuendo, and rude remarks are all signs that this person has resorted to bullying instead of actual facts. These bullying tactics work. They rile you up, they make you chuckle, you might even cheer them on, but that is how bullying has always worked. And bullying tactics are a constant reminder of us vs. them mentality. It reaffirms to our allies that we are better than those people we are insulting and it assures our enemies of the imbedded hatred towards them. Just like any other marketing tactic, it is used because it works.

3.15 Although this meme is trying to make a point it ends with name calling. No one is going to listen to you if you call them names. This meme remains a failed rebuttal to his actions because of what was written in the last line.

Classic bullying tactics can also go beyond aggressive language and insults. It can include batching a group together with extremists. It can include discrimination in the name of religion or other causes. Whenever one group of people is being targeted overly aggressively, you can always think of that as bullying.

Many see this behavior as a sign of strength. But in reality it is overcompensation and a cry for attention. This attention riles people up and creates a mob mentality. The sheer momentum of bullying tactics makes for powerful distractions as a way to avoid facts that don't support the bully's stance. Remember those who sling mud are actually losing the ground they stand on.

3.16 Us vs. Them Language

Us, we, all of us, like us, like you, with me, and other phrases that put you in the same group as the person speaking are inclusive and make us feel like part of a group. We feel solidarity, loyalty, and like we are connected with the speaker. These phrases are constantly used by public figures when drumming up support for their political agenda. But these type of language cues almost always have reaffirming 'them' type language that follows. *Them, others, they, those people, people like them,* and other more aggressive phrases demeaning a group. Thes words intentionally make others a threat, and are almost always used to divide you emotionally from another group of people. It is amazing how easily this works. It usually is used in line with an already established bias. It reaffirms to the listener that they are an insider and the enemy is anyone who is not part of their group.

> *"As I grew up, I thought abuse like this would happen less and less. But I was wrong. Adults try to create outsiders, too. In fact, we get better at it. And most of us fall into the same three groups: the people who try to create outsiders, the people who are made to feel like outsiders, and the people who stand by and don't stop it."*
>
> - Melinda Gates
>
> *The Moment of Lift*

This classic divide and conquer tactic is often used in highly polarizing issues. We are pitched the problem as 'us vs. them' instead of 'us all vs. the problem' coming up with different solutions. While we continually fight one another we spend almost no energy actually fighting the problem. This helps maintain the status quo. Keeping your energy targeted at a group of people over the actual problem guarentees limited resources will go towards an issue. You see this in all kinds of hot button issues from women's rights to gun control. And as long as they can convince you that other people working on the problem are the enemy, or that you are a victim of their solution, you will put all your energy toward fighting them instead of the actual problem.

This tactic is one of the easiest to spot once we learn to identify it. It becomes almost comical hearing political figures creating divisions of people with their language. They put people into unnecessary groups and create tribal like rivalry for their own benefit. It is astonishing how people eat it up. Watching as people cheer on and even contribute to this propaganda without even realizing they are being told to create an enemy out of someone they could actually combine forces with is a scary glimpse into mob mentality.

3.17 Political Buzzwords

You can also think of these as common political phrases that have huge baggage wrapped into the words' meaning based on current discourse in popular culture. Sometimes they are name-calling words like: bigot, Moscow Mitch, snowflake, libtard, feminazi, Killary, or Commander and Cheeto. Sometimes they are loaded political jargon that people tend to misuse like: 'witch hunt,' 'communist,' 'fake news,' 'fascist,' 'socialist,' 'invasion,' and 'Nazi.' Sometimes they are just repeated sayings that mean more than what they say, like: "build the wall," "gun stealing liberal," "lock her up," or "drain the swamp."

These phrases truly are so loaded that they stir really strong polar reactions. If you think about political buzzwords or phrases a little more deeply, you will realize they are focusing on target markets. They have basically become widely used marketing slogans. They are also so commonly improperly used (yes, I am saying people don't know what these phrases actually mean) that they aren't all that helpful in conversations when used between people of differing political affiliations. They tend to be very fast ways for polarized opinions to shut down any real logical conversations, depending on what side of the topic they are on. If someone is just parroting this kind of political jargon they aren't really being helpful on the topic.

3.18 Suggestibility, Shadow of Doubt, Implying, or Alleging

One of the slimiest ways to say something and not be held accountable is to hint at it. "I hear that ... " "Trusted sources say ... " and "I'm not saying it is but ... " are all classic ways to tell a lie and not be held accountable for it. These suggestions are enough to plant ideas in people's heads that are ludicrous. But it also gives public figures a way out if there is backlash. They can always claim they never said that!

These marketing tactics target people who are drawn to conspiracy theories or distrust the world around them. Once you plant the seed of a possible hidden truth, you have waves of people who will stack on to that idea and carry your message far and wide. And the public figure can claim no responsibility for the repercussions.

3.19 People Just Like Me

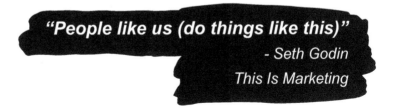

"People like us (do things like this)"

- Seth Godin

This Is Marketing

We are far more likely to identify with someone who we perceive to be just like us or just like the person we believe we could be. When a political figure tries to be relatable, they are giving the false impression that they were once just like us and rose from the ranks through hard work and perseverance (trust me, luck and money will never be mentioned) and are still just like us.

Constituents often vote against their own interests purely to stay in the political group they have always identified with. The person who votes against their own self-interest does so to maintain a feeling of community, belonging, self-identity, and to reaffirm past life choices. That sense of self and belonging is far more valuable than any of the actual political ideas. We will search for all kinds of 'facts' to reaffirm these feelings of belonging and when presented with contrary evidence we will most likely double down on the stance that aligns with our identity. Belonging is an extremely powerful marketing tool.

3.20 Social Proof

Social proof is a fancy way of saying "Everyone else thought it was a good idea." Social proof online comes in the form of clicks, likes, shares, and comments. The more friends you see sharing and liking something, the more you will be convinced it is the right thing to share. We all want to be liked, and social proof has been ingrained in us since we were kids because we all want to fit in. Marketers use every single tool they can to get social proof on a post because that snowballing effect is invaluable. The problem is social proof is more based on algorithms, marketing tactics, and herd mentality than any actual proof of anything.

As you read all of these following marketing tactics, ask yourself how many of them could be a kind of social proof?

3.21 Short and Simple

Yup, it is the Keep It Simple Stupid (KISS) tactic again. But pay attention to this. Short and simple is why memes work. Short and simple is why headlines work. And short and simple is why tweets go viral. In fact, most marketing copy in e-mails and social media posts are written at a fifth-grade reading level and below.

If a political issue is complex, keep that in mind when we see a very simple explanation. That is a marketing tactic and we deserve more information and are smart enough to understand the issue in full.

3.22 The Humorous Retort

Humor is an obvious marketing tactic, but combine that with sticking it to our rivals and it becomes viral gold! The humorous retort is a major political marketing tactic. We all love to think we are smarter than other people, and what better way to show that than a meme on the Internet that clearly solves this whole situation?!? (This is sarcasm, but this is actually how it plays out.)

So much of what is shared online is snide commentary on a subject. But what is seen as humor from our vantage point is most likely an insult or bullying toward someone else. We were the meme's target market. It was made for people like us to share. Just remember that it was made to make us think we are funny or right, and it is our own selfish aggrandizement and satisfaction that got us to share and create more animosity and division.

Donald J. Trump ✓
@realDonaldTrump

Happy New Year to all, including to my many enemies and those who have fought me and lost so badly they just don't know what to do. Love!

12/31/16, 7:17 AM

Do better bruh.

3.22 Instead of wishing the country a Happy New Year, the President-elect chose to be petty and post snide commentary. His use of this kind of retort is so common that his supporters justify this bad behavior and absolve him from all responsibility for his remarks by stating, "That is just how he talks."

3.23 Made-Up Stories

Stories are how the human mind comprehends information. Our minds can often get tricked when we are told stories that are oversimplified examples or made-up tropes. It is a way to present the exact made-up logic needed to market an idea while avoiding all the logic that doesn't support it. Politicians use made-up stories all the time. And when they do, we should always ask ourselves why? The reason is because they can tell a made-up story in a way that is beneficial to their cause.

Take the example of the political fairy tale made up by Sarah Huckabee Sanders about journalists drinking in a bar. This oversimplified metaphor was used to 'logically' explain the new tax plan. But you can follow logic anywhere you want to go. It is your fairy tale and you can take it anywhere you want to. I knew people who argued vehemently that this story was all logic and represented college-level economics. That is how powerful a story can be. Tropes like paid protesters, welfare queens, lazy immigrants, and immigrants taking our jobs have been ingrained in us so deep that even if we are given a real contradicting example, we will believe the anecdotal story.

If politicians make up a fictional story to explain an idea, remember that our brains will follow their logic because stories are how our brains understand the world around us. We are programmed to learn with stories even if they are made-up.

3.24 Exaggeration and Superlative Language

All of these techniques are basically people lying, but getting out of it because of a technicality. I am all for these tactics in fiction writing, in retail marketing, and in casual conversation, but in politics, they are lies.

If a politician talks about thousands of terrorists coming over the border and there aren't thousands of terrorists coming over the border, then they aren't just exaggerating. They are lying.

Superlative language has now become ingrained in political discourse and this again is lying. Superlative language is used constantly when marketing retail products: "The BEST cleaner money can buy!" "The GREATEST hair care product on the market." The BIGGEST discount EVER in our store's history." It is a great way to sell a product, but it isn't truthful. It is marketing. It goes into a subjective gray area of pushing what can be said about a product without being sued. But in politics the results of legislation and policy are quantitative and not subjective. If a politician claims they passed the BEST legislation for protecting the environment and it actually isn't, they are lying. If a politician claims to have the GREATEST voting record on Medicare and they actually don't, they are lying. And if a politician claims they gave us the BIGGEST tax cut EVER in history and it actually isn't ... They. Are. Lying.

3.25 Implied Victories

Implied victories are tricky. Sometimes they sound like promises people might not be able to keep. But most of the time they talk about victories that 'could have' happened if not for other people getting in the way. This fuels resentment in followers of what could have been. Most of the time the politician swears they did everything they should have, boasts about it as if it was an actual achievement, and then blames the failure on anyone but themselves. It can be something as simple as claiming that their speech could have filled a larger venue, or the entire nation was going to be better off because of everything they did.

This tactic reminds me of the kid in class that brags about how well he was going to do on the test because he is smarter than everyone else in class, then when he gets a poor score, he says it was because his hand cramped or the room was cold. And if his hand felt normal and the room wasn't cold, it would have been his best grade ever! He never once brings up the fact that he didn't study and this caused him to fail. He keeps the glory and places any failure on external factors—a classic marketing spin on the truth.

What is so tricky about this marketing tactic is it gives you warm adoration for the person as if they really accomplished the things they are talking about. It tricks your brain into giving them your trust as if it already happened. It is misplaced trust.

3.26 Placing the Blame

Placing the blame goes hand in hand with implied victories. It is always the other party's fault! Am I right? The minute I hear someone saying it is entirely the other party's fault, I basically glaze over. Placing the blame on someone or something else abdicates any responsibility for failure on your side. My favorite example of placing blame was how everything that went wrong from 2017-2018 was all the Democrats' fault despite the GOP having control of the House, Senate, and White House. How can having two years of complete control of all three branches of government, resulting in not having a new healthcare system in place, and not having the US-Mexico wall somehow be the Democrats' fault?

Placing blame can be far more retroactive than anyone could possibly imagine. Years later, people are still blaming current conditions on past elected officials. So much so that 'Thanks Obama' has become sort of a running joke across our country.

3.27 Grassroots and Elitists

Everyone wants to feel like they helped tip the scale and were part of a grassroots movement. It makes us feel important. It is those other people who are elitists. This is such a common marketing trope in politics that its cliché use almost makes me gag.

On the flip side of this, someone who has a special club or group they are proud to belong to is basically the definition of an elitist. You can even be an elitist insider of a grassroots movement! Both grassroots camaraderie and elitist accusations are potent marketing tactics and when you learn to recognize how often politicians use them, you will roll your eyes right along with me.

3.28 Victimhood

> *"We suffer more in imagination than in reality."*
> - Seneca

Pay attention if a public figure tells you that you are somehow a victim. Victimhood marketing also shows up as one group deserving better treatment than others due to some demographic factor. Victimhood marketing has become so common that many conservative talk shows have earned the nickname 'victim radio.' I find this to be one of the most terrifying political marketing trends I have seen in the past few years, because I have seen the hostility and visceral anger it generates when people believe they are a victim. I mainly see this play out when people protest injustices. Often protests of wrongful deaths or discrimination are met with the opposing side saying they are now the victim and feel disrespected. It is a natural reaction when someone presents us with the idea that we have been complicit in maintaining a hurtful status quo. Examining how we might be part of systemic problems is painful. But confronting that discomfort, acknowledging our responsibility, and trying to change is far more heroic than deciding you are now somehow the victim as you draw a line in the sand to stay exactly where you are.

Politicians, political commentators, and trolls have become experts at leveraging victimhood. But the truth on whether something actually affects us vs. makes us uncomfortable is an extremely trying realization to come to. And if a politician standing on a podium reaffirms that we are the real victim, we will claim we are being abused by the other side and demand they stop confronting us on the issue. Trevor Noah, host of *The Daily Show,* does an amazing job explaining the leveraging of victimhood in an online episode of his *Between the Scenes* series where he comments on current issues. He talks about how the gift of victimhood from politicians is given to those who are often the least deserving.

3.29 Religious Marketing

> *"I distrust those people who know so well what God wants them to do, because I notice it always coincides with their own desires."*
>
> -Susan B. Anthony

Religion being used in politics is target marketing like anything else. It is focused on a certain group of people who find religion comforting. It is almost always a Christian focused type of religeous marketing used in United States politics. But most don't notice it because they have grown up in the dominant culture for so long they take it for granted that it can make many people uncomfortable.

Most religions have some form of higher power, holy texts, codes of conduct, rituals, and prayers/chants, but just hearing the terms described through the terminology of a different religion can provoke real discomfort. An easy way to understand how religion in politics can be offensive and alienating to those of a different religion is by swapping out the religious nomenclature and see how it feels to you. Would you be offended if American currency said "In Allah We Trust?" Would you be bothered if someone quoted the Torah for their reason for moving forward with a certain piece of legislation? Would you feel uncomfortable if someone said they wanted to start the meeting with everyone holding hands and doing a Shamanic chant?

We will never know whose religion is right, but we do know exactly which market is being targeted when religion is used in politics. If there are two things we all agree on, we believe we are the good drivers on the road and the other guy is the bad driver, and we believe our religion is the right one while the rest have it wrong. It is the blatant disregard for what others hold as true that creates so much blowback when religion is used to market political ideas (not to mention the cherry-picking of ideas that are referenced to align with specific political agendas). I know pastors who are extremely liberal and I know pastors who are extremely conservative from the same denominations. We can all interpret scripture in the way we want and that has to be acknowledged. So the next time it feels like something is absolute blasphemy going against your beliefs, try to remember they are *your* beliefs. And despite being able to cite how your religion directly aligns with your beliefs, someone from the exact opposite viewpoint who has your same religion can probably do the same.

> Don't buy the new Pepsi can
> coming out with pics of the
> Empire State building and
> the Pledge of Allegiance on
> them. Pepsi left out 2
> little words in the pledge:
> "Under God." Pepsi said
> they didn't want to offend
> anyone. So if we don't buy
> them, they won't be
> offended when they don't
> receive our money with the
> words "In God We Trust" on
> it. How fast can u repost

3.29 I see a version of this meme in my social feeds often. It is specifically targeted to Christians that believe their religion is offensive to others and under attack. The problem is this never happened. There was never a Pepsi can like this. There was once a Dr. Pepper can that had the words "ONE NATION ... INDIVISIBLE" written on it but it had no other words. It only included three. This was not a religious slight. But this meme keeps popping up because it reinforces the idea of victimhood to its target market. In Talking Across the Divide: How to Communicate with People You Disagree with and Maybe Even Change the World *author Justin Lee talks about an in-person altercation with a woman who swore up and down it was real and he was lying. That is the power of seeing information over and over reinforcing things that aren't true. The women probably even created the picture of the can in her head and absolutely believed the fantasy to be true.*

3.30 People Suck at Numbers

People are bad with numbers. Yes, even you. It is how our brains work. That is why numbers are used by marketing all the time. And this works amazingly well with online political marketing. Numbers are used to turn people against those less fortunate, they are used to make people feel they are victims, and numbers are used in grand gestures to make things seem highly impactful when not taken into full context. When numbers are leveraged in marketing tactics, there are three main ways they trick us:

People have a hard time picturing big numbers

Our brains can't actually conceptualize big numbers. It is why we spend time squabbling over a $15 minimum wage but don't get mad when a CEO makes $37 million a year. It is because our brains can picture what $15 an hour is. But they have no grasp on what making $37 million a year is.

People don't understand numbers in a larger context

Our brains will follow logic wherever we want it to go. If numbers are presented to us in a way that supports our side, we will believe the information is infallible. Let's say you live in a town of one-hundred people. Let's say ten people got speeding tickets the last quarter. Five of them went to people who were white and five went to people of color. Seems fair, right? But what if there are only ten people of color in the entire town? Now in the larger context of the population demographics, something is really wrong.

3.30.1 I saw this image spread like wildfire when people we arguing the validity of Black Lives Matter. This was supposed to support the argument that less black people are killed by police than white people. But in fact it does the

exact opposite. If black deaths were equal in frequency to white deaths than the numbers should represent population percentages where blacks make up about 12% of our country's population and whites make up about 76%. The number of blacks killed by police should represent this population proportion if there was no bias. The number of black deaths should be closer to 50 as compared to 326 white deaths. Instead this shows blacks are killed over twice the rate of whites when you consider the larger context of total population. People sharing it were undermining their own point but still thought this proved their point.

The larger context is something that is misunderstood more often than not. It plays out so often when you take information at face value and don't ask yourself about other key factors that are needed to clearly see the entire picture. You also see this in grand gestures when people donate large amounts of money to a cause but really it is just a drop in the bucket to them.

People readily believe numbers that feel anecdotally true

We are more apt to question numbers when it goes against our beliefs. But if a number lines up with our confirmation bias and what we anecdotally believe to be true, we won't give it a second thought. We will accept it to be truth with no links to proof of the numbers.

3.30.2 It doesn't matter how true I believe these numbers to be. I saw this meme shared over and over and it never included links to the numbers it claimed to represent. Without links I need to fight my personal assumption that these feel like they would be true.

3.31 The Story of One

It is really hard to relate to large problems. But it is easy to relate to one person. A great example of this is how charities feature stories of people they help when they ask for financial support. They often say things like "Help more children like Ben ... " because it is easier to create empathy for an individual. Talking about the issue as if it is just about the one person is far more compelling than, "Help 500 children this year fight cancer." That is why when explaining an issue, many times politicians share the story of one person to highlight their point. This goes right back to the idea that people aren't good at picturing large numbers.

The main problem with the 'story of one' is politicians often choose an extreme example. The only time the 'story of one' should be relevant is if an example is of a consistent repeated pattern or statistic trend. If a statistical anomaly is being used to stir up support around a goal, you should look at the story as a marketing tactic. Also, Trump has been known to tell the same 'story of one' featuring a person in the story whose name changes each time. This makes these particular stories most likely made up to fit into the story of one marketing tactic.

3.31 Mollie Tibbetts' murder was politicized as a 'story of one' by the Trump administration to support building a border wall because the man who murdered her was in the country illegally. Statistically what happened was an anomaly not a pattern and the family did not want their daughter's death used this way. Despite the family's wishes memes like this are permanently memorializing their daughter on the Internet with words against their beliefs.

3.32 The Grand Gesture

We should always be super conscious when we see someone making a grand gesture. Try to think of that person's ulterior motives. Why? Because they want us to think a certain way about them, and if that isn't marketing, then you have missed the point of this book! Marketing is changing perception and that is what a grand gesture attempts to do in one big flashy act.

Usually monetary grand gestures are the ones to be the most skeptical of and need us to think critically about. Whenever money is donated or someone works for free, we have to think about what impact this really made on their life. Are they using it as a tax write-off? Are they using it to appear like a big gesture but really it is a drop in the bucket compared to their income (remember people suck at large numbers)? Are they working for free to get around nepotism accusations or even worse—regulations and laws? When someone makes a grand gesture, be sure to consider it against the bigger picture and remember it is marketing. Even pay attention to photo ops in the right places, at the right time, with the right people or how public figures will 'help out' celebrities in their time of need. This guarentees press coverage for what they did.

3.33 Riding the Coattails

An amazing strategy to get attention is to find an event in the news and make it part of your cause. This strategy feels really lazy when you think about it, but boy does it work! Politicians will jump on any trend, any event, and any hashtag if they feel it will be beneficial to their cause. This can create some very unfortunate situations and publicity that private individuals didn't ask for.

3.34 Highlight Reels

Be wary of 'highlight reels.' Anytime we see content that has been clipped from something longer, assume we don't know the full context. Both liberals and conservatives use the highlight reel tactic to spin the words their opposition says on the record. If the quote in sliced video footage sounds awful, go back to the original transcript and read the entire account. Often the snippet isn't representative of the entire concept being conveyed. These misused quotes can often be used in articles, memes, and spread far and wide without context.

The next use of highlight reels are these terrifyingly effective doomsday/conspiracy theory videos and documentaries. They often use clip after clip of scary footage with snippets of quotes from angry politicians. They are often narrated and tell you a story their creators want to spin. They leverage fear and conspiracies to grip their audiences. I have seen people in a panic over these videos, believing wholeheartedly that they are real evidence. The graphic images, angry faces, and narration are created specifically to instill fear and hatred and stop any chance of rational thinking. They often feature subject experts no one has ever heard of (but hey—they are shown sitting in front of a bookshelf with fancy books) who are completely biased, and the entire video looks well produced.

3.35 Omittance Marketing/No Gray Areas

Sometimes not saying something is also a form of marketing strategy. When a politician sells an idea as having no room for compromise, there are two big reasons. The first is that it is far easier to market a simple, singular idea. Not only does it make the politician appear tough on the issue, but the KISS marketing tactic is in their favor and people are easily able to repeat their stance over and over and over and spread the information far and wide.

The second reason a politician will completely avoid a question about gray areas of a subject is because of the aforementioned highlight reels. If they are recorded backing away from their stance and their words are taken out of context, it is an asset for their opponents. Public figures are often asked questions that they respond to by pivoting their response so they don't actually answer the question, and this is completely intentional. By omitting their actual sentiments they are avoiding a highlight reel being used against them.

3.36 The False Positive

Biased or extreme leaning news outlets often blow participation in extreme opposition actions or beliefs out of proportion. This makes people believe that more people in their opposing political camp are involved than there really are. The illusion of opposition outrage or wider saturation of a fringe idea amongst the opposition is a form of marketing. Always compare what your media sources are presenting to what the opposition is actually doing or saying.

One of my favorite examples of this was when Brett Kavanaugh was being assessed for the Supreme Court. Many of my conservative friends were outraged by liberals sharing a gross cartoon featuring his child praying. They said it was everywhere, but when I asked them who they knew was sharing it, they couldn't think of one person. All they could come up with were news articles talking about the cartoon from far-right news outlets claiming it was being shared everywhere. The news articles said it was everywhere, and in their minds it became the true narrative.

I had never seen this political cartoon shared by any liberals I knew either, and wasn't even aware of it. When I Googled it, I came up with a bunch of far-right websites claiming liberals were sharing it everywhere. The articles featured posts from liberals that shared this cartoon and funny enough, all these different articles were citing the exact same people and the exact same posts. Apparently the meme that was seen 'everywhere' was only reported to be everywhere. This created the illusion that it was far more widespread than it really was.

3.37 Appearance and Aesthetics

Appearance and aesthetics are huge factors in the way people convince themselves content is true without having to look it up. We see something posted online and we think that visually it looks credible, so we don't fact-check it before passing the information along. The visual credibility of something has a great deal to do with people's life experiences. What looks credible to me may not look credible to you. We are all different target markets and the best marketing knows what will look credible to you. This is how phishing e-mail scams work—it looks real enough to get us to take the steps the scammer wants us to take.

The physical appearance of people online or on screen can also be a way of convincing people that content is right for them. Anytime there is a post that is negative about an individual, they will typically be pictured yelling with their mouth open or with some other negative expression on their face. If you are supposed to like someone, they will probably be smiling or looking noble. Marketing tactics that use appearance for positive or negative results can also make use of a person's race, type of clothing, and other physical attributes. *Fox News* is notorious for overwhelmingly featuring attractive white skinny blond women with big boobs. This is because they know it appeals to their target market, which is attracted to these types of women.

THIS IS AMERICA, LOVE IT OR LEAVE IT, SNOWFLAKE!

GAYS CAN GET MARRIED AND ADOPT CHILDREN, THAT'S THE LAW!

BROWN PEOPLE WERE HERE BEFORE US AND WILL BE HERE AFTER US, BETTER GET USED TO IT!

THE AFFORDABLE CARE ACT IS THE LAW, TOUGH SHIT, YOUR PREEXISTING CONDITIONS ARE COVERED!

IT'S ILLEGAL TO DISCRIMINATE BASED ON SEX, RACE, OR NATIONALITY. GO CRY ME A RIVER!

IF YOU DON'T LIKE IT, LEAVE. THIS IS AMERICA!

3.37 Online conservative imagery is notorious for having an aggressive faux patriotic aesthetic. They tend to have imagery of angry bald eagles, patriotic colors such as red white and blue color are everywhere, the American flag is overly used, they often combine guns or religion as other symbols of patriotism, and they tend to be aggresive and confrontational in feeling and in content.

The appearance of these memes go after the conservative target market and because that market is used to this kind of imagery they are more apt to trust it. Someone even made a meme mocking that style from the liberal viewpoint, tricking conservatives into reading it by mimicking the widely popular aggressive faux patriot aesthetic.

This makes me giggle.

64

3.38 Authority

Authority is as much a marketing tactic as it is a cultural norm that can be leveraged to benefit a political opinion. Those in authority positions are often quoted to back up opinions. Their statements have significant weight even if it is a lie because of the position they hold. These lies gain credibility simply by the perceived authority the figure has. And that perception is almost universal until someone finds cause to no longer trust that authority figure.

We have been trained since childhood that authority figures are right, have all the power, and not to question them because there will be consequences. We may find it hard to define authority, but if we walk into a room, we can instantly tell who the authority figures are because of societal norms we have been trained to recognize. White men have traditionally held higher positions of authority in our society. And when figures of traditional authority abuse their power, it is easy for them to sell the public that they are right, because our society is built to uphold the chain of command.

Our social conditioning on authority is a major factor why we blame the poor, vulnerable, or victims for a wide range of societal problems. We will guard the future life opportunities of an authority figure over those with less authority because it feels comfortable and we have been trained to do so.

When questioning an authority figure, you not only risk the wrath of the authority figure with power but the wrath of their following. Half the time the authority figure doesn't even have to acknowledge the confrontation because loyal followers are so reassured that their leader is in the right that they will enact their own form of vigilante justice. This can be truly terrifying because mob mentality can generate real harassment and violence in real life. When the president of the United States can stand at a podium and cheer on assaulting one of his constituents, we should all be terrified by the possible dangers of that kind of abuse of authority.

3.39 Authority Through Perceived Balance

Media caving to pressure to appear fair and balanced in news coverage has created this phenomenon that has run rampant. It often has a story with two 'experts' being interviewed with one representing each side of the issue. The only problem is with the 'experts.' Just because someone has an opinion that puts them on the opposite side of an issue doesn't make them an expert. Yet they are given equal airtime and equal opportunity to state their side to an audience. The perceived equality of these two gives one authority on the issue they shouldn't have.

Think about it in terms of an anti-vaxer and a scientist or a flat earther and someone from NASA. The only problem is it is almost never this easy to spot the person that doesn't have credibility. They probably have credentials that make them sound like an authority when they are introduced. This tactic has given authority and validity to arguments that honestly shouldn't get the time of day, all in the effort to appear balanced and fair. If you want a deeper discussion on this, Dan Rather goes into this problem more in his book *What Unites Us*.

This attempt at balance can also show up as not covering certain aspects of news to try to sound balanced. News outlets have been criticized for being against Trump for highlighting the strange rhetoric from the President. Many news sources have even stepped back from doing it to appear impartial. But this attempt at balance makes it appear that the status quo is acceptable and, unfortunately, isn't a real representation of what is actually happening or being said.

3.40 First Impressions Matter

The early bird really does get the worm. The first information you hear about a topic is pretty much going to cement your thoughts about it. Seriously, it is going to take a huge amount of counter evidence for you to reverse or revise that first opinion you formed. This is just how our brains work. And it is the reason the information gap between people of differing political opinions is so dangerous. It doesn't matter if the first information is a complete lie. If you heard it first, it will have a hold on you in a way no counter information ever will. Think about a person you got a bad first impression of but eventually changed your mind about. How long did it take and how many examples of them being a better person than you thought did it take for you to change your mind about them?

3.41 Lying

Yep, this goes without saying, but lying is a form of marketing. Lying is also a nicer way of saying propaganda. Lying is one of the easiest forms of marketing, because the truth takes research, a diverse range of perspectives, and integrity. Lying requires nothing but saying what you know will align with your agenda and move your cause forward. The same freedom of speech that protects you and me protects liars too. Yes, there absolutely are legal ramifications to certain lies. But lies flourish online with help from every single marketing tactic covered in this section. Often multiple tactics are used in a single viral post spreading a lie.

The most pivotal moment to stopping a lie is to cut it off right at the beginning. But preemptively preparing for whatever lies come out of a public figure's mouth is extremely hard to do, and no one is sitting next to a troll convincing them to stop making a false meme.

Lies also move faster than the truth. The truth takes research and can be complicated, and sometimes we don't even have the words to explain the truth. Lies don't have to be checked with anyone. If it sounds good, it is ready to spread.

Often times a lie by someone of authority is quoted as evidence and their authority makes us believe it to be true. And when it aligns with our confirmation bias, we genuinely think the information we are spreading is true. This confabulation has more and more people in earnest arguing that lies are real. That is the true power of a lie. It has the backing of people who sincerely and passionately believe it is true. This means far less people even see the truth and the lie lives on in a majority of the population it touched, even if it was proven false at some point. The damage is done by that first impression created by the propaganda.

3.42 Multiple Marketing Tactics in One

As I said before, once you see marketing tactics, it is extremely hard to unsee them. Look at what can be done with these examples. One e-mail, one meme, or one post can leverage multiple marketing tactics (in fact they usually do). Knowing the tactics shouldn't be the basis to changing your mind on the information you are being presented with, but it should give you insight as to what the marketing wants you to think and then you can make a more informed opinion.

Check out these following email examples of online marketing. They all use multiple tactics to get you to buy the ideals they are selling. I am going to show you four different emails and I am going to highlight the marketing tactics used. Once I point these marketing tactics out you can see exactly what they are trying to make you think.

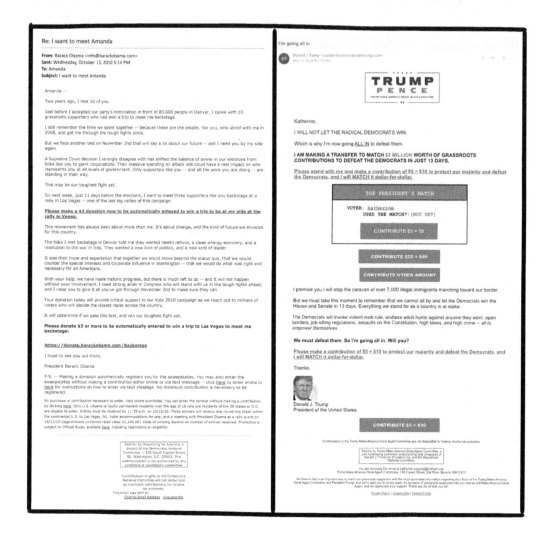

3.42.1 & 3.42.2

Both of these emails came from the campaigns of sitting Presidents in October two years after being elected. I am going to point out the marketing tactics used in these emails. Just so you are aware, the email from 2010 no longer has imagery available or had none at all but I don't know with certainty what the email looked like originally. The email was not sent to me so it addresses my friend Amanda who gave this email to me for reference.

I labeled the following emails with numbers to point out different marketing tactics used at specific points. Use the numbers to look back and reference where the tactic I am referring to is in the emails.

Re: I want to meet Amanda **(1.)**

From: Barack Obama <info@barackobama.com>
Sent: Wednesday, October 13, 2010 5:14 PM
To: Amanda
Subject: I want to meet Amanda **(2.)**

Amanda --

Two years ago, I met 10 of you. **(3.)**

Just before I accepted our party's nomination in front of 80,000 people in Denver, I spoke with 10 grassroots supporters who had won a trip to meet me backstage. **(4.)**

I still remember the time we spent together -- because these are the people, like you, who stood with me in 2008, and got me through the tough fights since. **(5.)**

But we face another test on November 2nd that will say a lot about our future -- and I need you by my side again. **(6.)**

A Supreme Court decision I strongly disagree with has shifted the balance of power in our elections from folks like you to giant corporations. Their massive spending on attack ads could have a real impact on who represents you at all levels of government. Only supporters like you -- and all the work you are doing -- are standing in their way. **(7.)**

This may be our toughest fight yet. **(8.)**

So next week, just 11 days before the elections, I want to meet three supporters like you backstage at a rally in Las Vegas -- one of the last big rallies of this campaign. **(9.)**

Please make a $3 donation now to be automatically entered to win a trip to be at my side at the rally in Vegas. **(10.)**

This movement has always been about more than me. It's about change, and the kind of future we envision for this country. **(11.)**

The folks I met backstage in Denver told me they wanted health reform, a clean-energy economy, and a resolution to the war in Iraq. They wanted a new kind of politics, and a new kind of leader. **(12.)**

It was their hope and expectation that together we would move beyond the status quo, that we would counter the special interests and corporate influence in Washington -- that we would do what was right and necessary for all Americans. **(13.)**

With your help, we have made historic progress, but there is much left to do -- and it will not happen without your involvement. I need strong allies in Congress who will stand with us in the tough fights ahead, and I need you to give it all you've got through November 2nd to make sure they can. **(14.)**

Your donation today will provide critical support to our Vote 2010 campaign as we reach out to millions of voters who will decide the closest races across the country. **(15.)**

It will determine if we pass this test, and win our toughest fight yet. **(16.)**

3.42.1

1. **Re: I want to meet Amanda** *title of this email is leveraging multiple tactics. The 'Re:' makes you think you might have sent an email prior to receiving this one which might make you more likely to open. It is also casual and is personalised using her first name only leveraging the 'Faking Authenticity and Personal Attention' tactic.*

3.42.1

2. *Notice it says her first name over and over again keeping it casual and again using the 'Faking Authenticity and Personal Attention' tactic.*

3. *The line:* **Two years ago, I met 10 of you** *is a variation on the 'Story of One' marketing tactic. By talking about only ten people it is much easier to picture.*

4. *This actually says* **grassroots supporters** *so it is clearly leveraging the 'Grassroots and Elitists' marketing tactic*

5. *This is another variation on the story of one and makes you feel more personally connected as it relates that these people are like you. It also employs 'Aggressive Language' with* **tough fights** *but the language isn't directly pointed at anyone or anything in particular.*

6. **I need you by my side again** *leverages 'Faking Authenticity and Personal Attention' along with 'Patriotism', and 'Guilt' marketing tactics.*

7. This clearly uses 'Grassroots and Elitists' marketing tactics pinning you the grassroots supporter against big businesses and decisions done in their favor by the Supreme Court

8. **This may be our toughest fight yet** is 'Aggressive Language' and tells you just whose side you are on with the 'Us vs. Them' tactic as well.

9. **I want to meet three supporters just like you** is the 'Story of One' again. you can picture that and you can picture yourself there.

10. We are then asked for a **$3 donation** for a chance to be one of those three people we pictured. The use of the number 3 is an example of 'Repetition'. By saying the number 3 over and over again it is now stuck in your head.

11. This sentence leverages 'Patriotism.'

12. **The folks I met backstage** has a casual feel and again uses the 'Story of One' and by continuing to repeat this story 'Repetition Makes the Heart Grow Fonder' and you more and more want to be one of those special people.

13. So many tactics here. 'Us vs. Them,' 'Grassroots,' 'Patriotism,' and 'Story of One' are all used here.

14. **I need strong allies in Congress who stand with us in tough fights** is an 'Us vs. Them' tactic and also uses 'Aggressive Language.'

15. **Your donation today will provide critical support to our Vote 2010 campaign** is creating a 'Sense of Urgency' for you to donate now with the deadline truly being arbitrary.

16. Again creates a 'Sense of Urgency' for you to donate now.

17. You are again asked to donate and 'Repetition Makes the Heart Grow Fonder' of this idea.

18. The sign-off is **President Barack Obama** to give it 'Authority' and 'Authenticity' but he did not write this email.

19. The **PS-** is a great strategy to get people to keep reading. It again asks for money using the 'Repetition' marketing tactic.

20. *This is disclaimer copy and not much marketing is happening here except the fact that it is smaller to make it less noticeable and unimportant.*

21. *This is mainly legal requirements at the end of an email and is made small because it is seen as unimportant and they want you to ignore it.*

The overall tactic of this email was 'Repetition Makes the Heart Grow Fonder' and the others were used to enforce this tactic. The point of this email was to remind you to donate again and again and to leverage other tactics to convince you to do so. The goal of raising funds is pretty standard for any political campaign email.

This email was also pretty casual. When reading it you felt like you were in a casual conversation. A few parts stuck out but nothing was really screaming at you or demanding you to participate. The marketing tactics were pretty passive overall and not too agressive or divisive.

Unfortunately, I can't comment on how this one looks visually not knowing what it originally looked like. So keep that in mind when I comment on the aesthetics of the next email because it won't be a true 1-to-1 comparison.

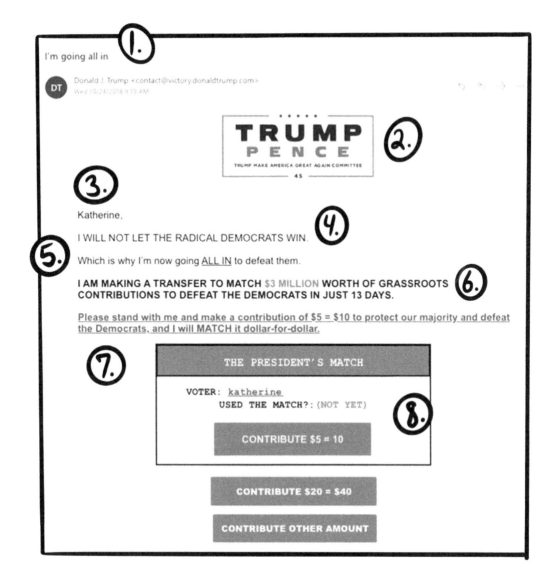

3.42.2

1. ***I'm going all in*** *is the title of this email uses 'Superlative Language' as well as implies a 'Grand Gesture.'*

2. *It is then branded with their campaign slogan which is visually very well designed incorporating red, white, and blue, and uses 'Nostalgia' in their tagline phrase.*

3. *This again is a personal salutation again using the 'Faking Authenticity and Personal Attention' tactic.*

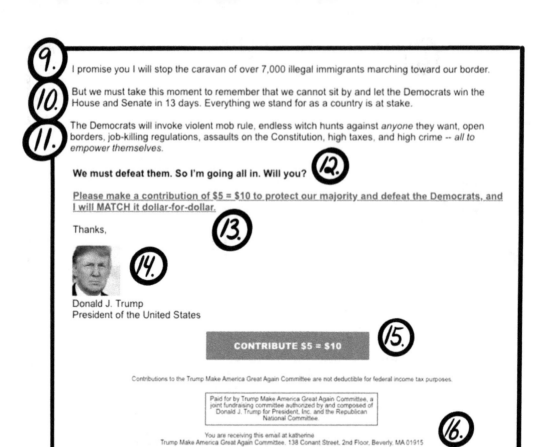

I promise you I will stop the caravan of over 7,000 illegal immigrants marching toward our border.

But we must take this moment to remember that we cannot sit by and let the Democrats win the House and Senate in 13 days. Everything we stand for as a country is at stake.

The Democrats will invoke violent mob rule, endless witch hunts against *anyone* they want, open borders, job-killing regulations, assaults on the Constitution, high taxes, and high crime -- *all to empower themselves.*

We must defeat them. So I'm going all in. Will you?

<u>Please make a contribution of $5 = $10 to protect our majority and defeat the Democrats, and I will MATCH it dollar-for-dollar.</u>

Thanks,

Donald J. Trump
President of the United States

CONTRIBUTE $5 = $10

3.42.2

4. *This is where it starts to get complicated...* **I WILL NOT LET THE RADICAL DEMOCRATS WIN** *is in all caps which makes it 'Aggressive Language' and reads like it is yelling. It also instantly tells you whose side you are on because the use of 'Name Calling' tells you it is 'Us vs. Them' and the Democrats are the enemy that must be defeated.*

5. *This is 'Repetition Makes the Heart Grow Fonder' by repeating the beginning 'Superlative' 'Grand Gesture' statement used in the title of the email. It is also 'Aggressive Language' again leveraging all caps and uses 'Us vs. Them' by saying* **<u>ALL IN</u> to defeat them.** *You know exactly who the enemy is, and he is claiming he will do anything to beat them.*

6. *This section is 'Aggressive Language' and is claiming a 'Grand Gesture' by implying he is personally donating money by saying* **I AM MAKING A TRANSFER**. *It also leverages 'Grassroots and Elitists' by saying* **GRASSROOT CONTRIBUTIONS**.

*Now let's talk about the **MATCH**. I haven't mentioned this marketing tactic in the book as of yet. But having worked in the nonprofit sector for almost a decade I know a lot about them. Matches are leveraged all the time by fundraising to increase donations. It even works on me! But in reality they are a marketing tactic like anything else and many aren't exactly honest. Many times the money given as a match would be given regardless of your donation. Your money didn't actually help get that other money because the large matching donation was never contingent on your donation. It is all just marketing to create a 'Sense of Urgency' and it markets that one 'Grand Gesture' donating that will inturn make your contribution a 'Grand Gesture' too, by falsely inflating your impact.*

Sometimes matches are real, but the wording has to be very specific and talk about how the money will not be received unless you give first to unlock the larger match donation. If it is just referenced as a match without any contingencies it is most likely just a marketing term to make you donate because you think you are magically giving more. But you aren't. Someone else gave money and despite being told your contribution is now more it really isn't. [3.42.2.1]

7. *This section is reiterating the match language and is using 'Repetition'.*

8. *This section leverages 'Authority' by titling it* **THE PRESIDENT'S MATCH**. *It is also using 'Faking Authenticity and Personal Attention' by using my name and my email. It also used 'Guilt' by labeling me personally in red as* **(NOT YET)** *referring to my lack of donation. It then uses 'Repetition' by giving me multiple buttons to donate.*

9. **I promise you I will stop the caravan of over 7,000 illegal immigrants marching toward our border** *has lots of tactics. The promise statement is a type of 'Implied Victory' and the issue of illegal immigrants leverages 'Fear' and 'Hatred.' The word marching is specifically used to leverage 'Fear' because this is a term of synchonized movement you would describe being used by an army, not families with with their small children in tow. It also is an 'Us vs. Them' tactic by pitting you against the immigrants.*

10. *This uses 'Us vs. Them' and 'Patriotism.'*

11. *This is the part of the e-mail that has me absolutely horrified. This is extremely 'Aggressive Language' and uses 'Us vs. Them' to pit you against Democrats. The kind of language used here is wartime propoganda. It is insinuating the retaliation will be violence and the language used makes threats against your personal safety. We really have to look at the entire thing because it is by far the best and most terrifying marketing in this e-mail.*

The Democrats will invoke violent mob rule, endless witch hunts against anyone they want, job-killing regulations, assaults on the Constitution, high taxes, and high crime -- all to empower themselves.

The entire sentence is strategically written to harness 'Fear.' The words **violent mob rule, witch hunts, assaults,** *the use of the word* **killing** *in* **job-killing,** *and* **high crime** *were all used purposefully to suggest the threat of violence. The words* **invoke, regulations, endless witchunts against** *anyone* **they want, high taxes,** *and* **all to empower themselves** *were specifically used to make you feel like your life would be out of your control. And feeling out of control causes even more 'Fear.' When you are fearful for your physical well-being and your family's physical well-being your 'Instinctive Thinking' takes over.*

But it is just one email right? Wrong. This messaging is just one example, but it has the 'Authority' of the highest office in our nation and this same rhetoric is used over and over at rallies, in tweets, in memes, in e-mails and in 'Repetition' unfortunately. The idea that you are in absolute danger from this enemy means there is no reasoning with you. Ever. And hell, if I were that scared there would be no reasoning with me either.

But why is this so bad? Why am I making such a big deal out of this? Because this kind of messaging is changing how we think. It is making us react as our worst selves not our best selves. And I have seen it play out in my life. I was talking to a coworker about a conversation she had with her mother-in-law and the mother-in-law was very worried about her living in such a liberal city with violent liberal mobs. My eyes got so wide because I realized I had gotten this email from the Trump campaign earlier that week with this exact ridiculous threatening language. This rhetoric put enough fear in a woman to make her believe her family was in danger and to check on them. If that woman was that scared do you think she would ever even listen to any progressive idea? Of course she wouldn't, because anything progressive now feels like a mortal threat from an enemy and she will do anything she can to avoid, dismiss, and retaliate against that enemy.

12. *This section is reiterating 'Us vs. Them' and the 'Grand Gesture' because 'Repetition Makes the Heart Grow Fonder.'*

13. *This is exactly the same tactics used as in 12, but worded differently.*

14. *To give the email 'Authority' and 'Authenticity' the sign-off is* **Donald J. Trump, President of the United States** *but he did not write this email.*

The photo of him is also used for recognition because as a TV actor his image is also part of 'Repetition Makes the Heart Grow Fonder.'

15. *They again ask for money because 'Repetition Makes the Heart Grow Fonder.'*

16. *And interestingly enough at the bottom they aren't just burying disclaimer copy. They must know that their target market will read it or that it had subliminal effect because they continue marketing even there. They leverage 'Grassroots and Elitists' yet again and mentions the President multiple times to remind them of his 'Authority' and thank the supporters repeatedly because 'Repetition.'*

Overall this email relied most heavily on 'Us vs. Them' and the 'Grand Gesture' and used 'Repetition' to really drive home these points. The point of this email was to remind you to donate again and again and to leverage other tactics to convince you to do so. The goal of raising funds is standard for any political campaign email.

Unfortunately, this email was divisive and threatening at best and wartime propaganda at worst. When reading it I felt alarm and my bullshit detector instantly went off because no one should try to put 'Fear' in me to accomplish their marketing goals.

I also have some real concerns about what this email visually looked like. The President can obviously make an email look however they want and this one looks like a Word document. That aesthetic is intentional, and since marketers double down on what works they know that having a shoddy looking email helps them appear 'Authentic' and more 'Grassroots.' It also mimics the aesthetic of really badly made divisive memes in appearace and language. This way it all blends together.

And that is terrifying because if a third-rate meme resembles White House communication the 'Aesthetic' gives it 'Authority' because it makes it almost indistinguishable from official communication. And this makes it harder for consumers to tell what is official and what isn't. But if unofficial sources are spreading your divisive messaging it is brilliant marketing to make them look similar. You now have an aesthetically coordinated campaign of division and misinformation aligned with trolls by making official communications look more amateur.

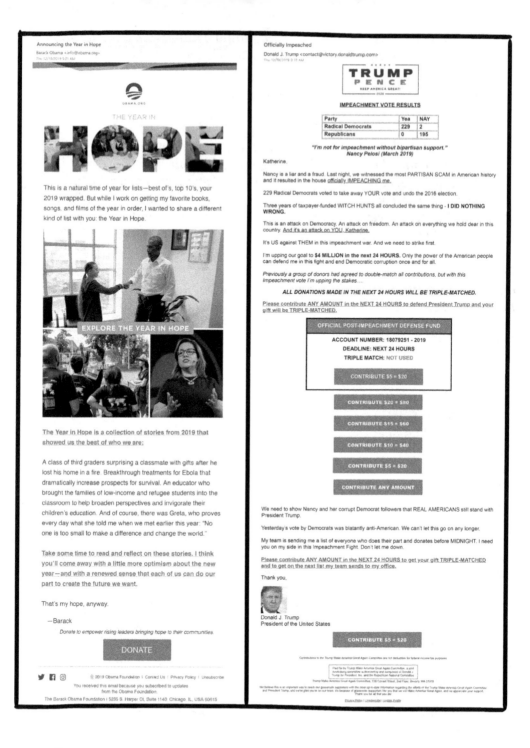

3.42.3 & 3.42.4

Both of these emails came on December 19, 2019. While they have different agendas they both are political in nature and you can compare the marketing tactics used in real time. I again labeled the following emails with numbers for you to reference the tactic I am referring to in the images of the emails.

①

②

OBAMA.ORG

THE YEAR IN

③

This is a natural time of year for lists—best of's, top 10's, your 2019 wrapped. But while I work on getting my favorite books, songs, and films of the year in order, I wanted to share a different kind of list with you: the Year in Hope.

④

EXPLORE THE YEAR IN HOPE

⑤

The Year in Hope is a collection of stories from 2019 that showed us the best of who we are:

A class of third graders surprising a classmate with gifts after he lost his home in a fire. Breakthrough treatments for Ebola that dramatically increase prospects for survival. An educator who brought the families of low-income and refugee students into the classroom to help broaden perspectives and invigorate their children's education. And of course, there was Greta, who proves every day what she told me when we met earlier this year: "No one is too small to make a difference and change the world."

Take some time to read and reflect on these stories. I think you'll come away with a little more optimism about the new year—and with a renewed sense that each of us can do our part to create the future we want.

That's my hope, anyway.

—Barack

Donate to empower rising leaders bringing hope to their communities.

> DONATE

3.42.3

1. *The beginning of this email starts off cheesy with the title **Announcing the Year in Hope** and with a brightly colored top border. 'Repetition Makes the Heart Grow Fonder' is used by having the word **Hope** in the title referencing back to Obama's presidential campaign.*

2. *The Obama.org logo is faded back in gray to highlight the beautifully vivid word **HOPE**. This is repetition from the title of the email and the photos show lots of diversity and smiling faces.*

3. *This has a little 'Grassroots' feel because you have to be in Obama's 'Target Market' to know his lists of favorite books, songs, and films of the year are coming. It again uses 'Repetition' by repeating the title of the email.*

4. *This image is an example of 'The Story of One' and 'Authority' because Greta Thunberg has become the international symbol of the younger generation speaking up for protecting the planet we are leaving them.*

5. *The next images and **EXPLORE THE YEAR IN HOPE** allude to the people speaking up for change in the images. It looks to be highlighting different versions of 'The Story of One' that you can check out. It again uses 'Repetition' by repeating the title of the email.*

6. *This again has 'Grassroots and Elitists' with **showed us the best of who we are** and also alludes to the upcoming stories that will provide you with 'Social Proof' of their mission and again uses 'Repetition' by repeating the title.*

7. *This entire paragraph talks about multiple 'Stories of One' that they want you to go read. Each one of them is 'Social Proof' of their mission. And the paragraph highlights 'Grassroots' by quoting Greta about how **No one is too small to make a difference and change the world** and it also drops her name again for 'Authority' and 'Authenticity.'*

8. *This again encourages you to check out their 'Stories of One' for the 'Social Proof' of their mission and encourages a 'Grassroots' attitude **with each of us can do our part**.*

9. *'Repetition' of the email theme is used and the signoff is just −**Barack** which is casual and gives it 'Authenticity' but still 'Authority' despite him most likely never writing or even seeing this email.*

10. *The ending uses 'Repetition' and instills the idea that donations will help uplift 'Grassroots' efforts. There is nothing standing out in disclaimer.*

Overall this email wants you to read their 'Stories of One' of their impact for 'Social Proof' of their mission. It uses lots of repetition, positivity, and images of happy people to make you feel uplifted and encouraged to learn more. It is a conversation about positive change and your 'Grassroots' contribution. Donations are not a high priority.

① Officially Impeached

Donald J. Trump <contact@victory.donaldtrump.com>
Thu 12/19/2019 9:13 AM

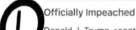

②

KEEP AMERICA GREAT!
2020

IMPEACHMENT VOTE RESULTS

Party	Yea	NAY
Radical Democrats	229	2
Republicans	0	195

④

"I'm not for impeachment without bipartisan support."
Nancy Pelosi (March 2019)

③

Katherine,

⑤ Nancy is a liar and a fraud. Last night, we witnessed the most PARTISAN SCAM in American history and it resulted in the house officially IMPEACHING me.

229 Radical Democrats voted to take away YOUR vote and undo the 2016 election. **⑥**

⑦ Three years of taxpayer-funded WITCH HUNTS all concluded the same thing - **I DID NOTHING WRONG.**

⑧ This is an attack on Democracy. An attack on freedom. An attack on everything we hold dear in this country. And it's an attack on YOU, Katherine.

It's US against THEM in this impeachment war. And we need to strike first. **⑨**

⑩ I'm upping our goal to **$4 MILLION in the next 24 HOURS.** Only the power of the American people can defend me in this fight and end Democratic corruption once and for all.

Previously a group of donors had agreed to double-match all contributions, but with this **⑪** *Impeachment vote I'm upping the stakes….*

ALL DONATIONS MADE IN THE NEXT 24 HOURS WILL BE TRIPLE-MATCHED.

Please contribute ANY AMOUNT in the NEXT 24 HOURS to defend President Trump and your gift will be TRIPLE-MATCHED.

⑫

OFFICIAL POST-IMPEACHMENT DEFENSE FUND

ACCOUNT NUMBER: 18079251 - 2019
DEADLINE: NEXT 24 HOURS
TRIPLE MATCH: NOT USED

CONTRIBUTE $5 = $20

CONTRIBUTE $20 = $80

CONTRIBUTE $15 = $60

CONTRIBUTE $10 = $40

CONTRIBUTE $5 = $20

CONTRIBUTE ANY AMOUNT

We need to show Nancy and her corrupt Democrat followers that REAL AMERICANS still stand with President Trump.

Yesterday's vote by Democrats was blatantly anti-American. We can't let this go on any longer.

My team is sending me a list of everyone who does their part and donates before MIDNIGHT. I need you on my side in this Impeachment Fight. Don't let me down.

<u>Please contribute ANY AMOUNT in the NEXT 24 HOURS to get your gift TRIPLE-MATCHED and to get on the next list my team sends to my office.</u>

Thank you,

Donald J. Trump
President of the United States

CONTRIBUTE $5 = $20

1. This email starts out saying **Officially Impeached** so I assume that is the subject of the email.

2. It again is branded with their campaign slogan which is visually very well designed with lots of red, white, and blue, and uses 'Nostalgia' in their tagline phrase. And then it has a chart of **IMPEACHMENT VOTE RESULTS** where 'Name calling' is used. It is only used towards **Radical Democrats** so you automatically know who the enemy is. Already you have been keyed into the idea that it is 'Us vs. Them' with the 'Aggressive Language' used against them before you even comprehend what is in the chart. The chart highlights the partisan vote which again is 'Us vs. Them.'

3. Next is a quote from Nancy Pelosi used as a 'Highlight Reel' and 'Social Proof' that the vote did not align with what she said. Making her original statement 'Lying' based on what actually happened to make the vote happen 9 months later.

4. This again is a personal salutation again using the 'Faking Authenticity and Personal Attention' tactic.

5. **Nancy is a liar and a fraud** is 'Name Calling' and from here on out the entire email is full of 'Agressive Language.' **the most PARTISAN SCAM in American History** is 'Superlative' and 'Aggressive' screaming about it and it ends with **IMPEACHING me** purposefully to leverage 'Victimhood' with **IMPEACHING** being large and shouted and **me** being small and passive. Think I am reaching on nitpicking this sentence? Imagine if this one line had been changed to: officially impeaching THE PRESIDENT OF THE UNITED STATES. It would have a totally different context. The President would have 'Authority' in the sentence. But in this case he doesn't want authority, he wants pity so it becomes the lowercase **me**.

6. This statement again has 'Name Calling' making it 'Us vs. Them' and makes you feel out of control and powerless in the situation which instills 'Fear.'

7. This uses the 'Political Buzzword' of **WITCH HUNTS**, which is also a 'False Analogy.' This word is a favorite when claiming 'Victimhood' however. It really misrepresents the situations it often refers to. In the United States we think of the Salem witch trials but the execution of burning primarily women for anything perceived as witchcraft/crime against Christianity goes even further back to King James (yes, that one whose popular edition of the Bible you might have heard of or own). The end of this statement **I DID NOTHING WRONG** is screaming 'Victimhood.'

8. The word attack is used with 'Repetition' and that kind of 'Aggressive Language' especially **it's an attack on <u>YOU</u>, *recipient's name*** is meant to make it feel 'Personal' and elicits 'Fear.'

9. Saying **US against THEM** is the clearest you can be with 'Us vs. Them' marketing tactics but the 'Agressive Language' of **war** and **strike first** is far more concerning because this is references of war-time violence.

10. This is a 'Grand Gesture' statement as well as 'Us vs. Them' and 'Aggressive Language' that refers to violence.

11. This is again a match-type offer. I am highly skeptical that it means anything besides being used to create a 'Sense of Urgency' and marketing the idea of a 'Grand Gesture' along with calls to 'Patriotism.'

12. Here they really lean on 'Repetition' with that arbitrary timeline to create a 'Sense of Urgency.'

13. Again the largest graphic is about donations. I now have an account number, the deadline is highlighted, and it feels like I am being tracked on some kind of spreadsheet with all the little factors.

14. And **NOT USED** is big and bold to stir up the feeling of 'Guilt' which is reinforced with that feeling of now being tracked by all those factors listed in the box.

15. So many ways to donate in 'Repetition' for this marketed match.

16. This is 'Us vs. Them' language again. It is also 'Aggressive Language' that leans on nationalism or 'Patriotism.'

17. This is a 'Repetition' of 'Us vs. Them' language again with 'Aggressive Language' that leans on nationalism.

18. This is making me feel 'Guilt' because the person of 'Authority' will see I didn't donate by the arbitrary date used to create a 'Sense of Urgency.' After his 'Grand Gesture' the least I can do is donate.

19. This is 'Repetition' of all the tactics used in the previous statement.

20. Again to give this email 'Authority' and 'Authenticity' the sign-off is **Donald J. Trump, President of the United States** but he did not write this email. The photo of him is also used for recognition because as a TV actor his image is also part of 'Repetition Makes the Heart Grow Fonder.'

21. *One last use of 'Repetition' to try to get money.*

22. *And again at the bottom they aren't just burying disclaimer copy. They know that their target market will read it or that it has a proven subliminal effect because they continue marketing even there. They leverage 'Grassroots and Elitists' yet again and mentions the President multiple times to remind them of his 'Authority' and thank the supporters repeatedly because 'Repetition.'*

3.42.3

Overall this email feels less agressive than the first one but it still deploys the kind of marketing tactics that instantly throw up alarm bells for me including the match promise that has so many matches it is almost comical and the use of 'Fear,' 'Aggressive Language,' and 'Victimhood.'

3.42.1 - 3.42.4

When I compare all these emails I know they have very different purposes for two very different audiences. And you can tell the Obama campaign email from 2010 is much closer to the Trump campaign emails with the goal of raising money. All of the emails that were sent as part of a presidential campaign really wanted my money more than anything. And the 2019 Obama email really was mission based and used to spread their accomplishments. Funding was not a top priority.

I hope you also emotionally felt a difference between these emails, because that is where real marketing lives. It lives in our emotions and how our brains truly work. There is a clear distinction in the way the Obama emails speak to their target market as compared to the Trump emails. And believe me the difference is intentional and is what works best to domineer the desired response of their target markets. The Obama emails feel more hopeful (yep, I just referenced the idea which was marketed to me) and are a call to do more collectively for our country, and the Trump emails rely on arbitrarily proclaiming/convincing his followers that you are the true America and any outsider who doesn't abide is an enemy and a threat to your actual well-being. The Trump e-mails make me fearful and make me feel guilty if I am not helping when an authority figure lays out such a grand gesture towards a subjectively defined 'true America.'

But it is just words, right? Yes, but these kind of messages and words are repeated over and over and each target market is fed their brand of marketing and it changes behavior. If I am told to be furious with someone for my own self-protection by my great leader I will use instinctive thinking in situations where my allegiance to what I perceive to be 'true America' is threatened. I don't want to be perceived as a weak link. I fear judgement. And this high level of emotion creates great attachment that brings into play victimhood and fearful reactions when my team is questioned. This heightened emotional state combined with the permission passed down by authority to use aggressive language freely towards the enemy to defend a discretionary stance is disastrous and has permeated throughout society.

So what marketing do you think truly helps you thrive? What marketing do you think is helpful for society as a whole? As you go through this entire book hold onto that question as you examine my examples and what you see marketed to you daily.

3.43 What Can You Do to Help?

Knowing these tactics will not only help you but they will help your friends and family when you hold yourself accountable about what you share online. Here are just a few tips you can enact right now that will help you be a more responsible consumer of online content:

1. Whenever you see information, keep in mind what marketing is being used to sway your opinion. This shouldn't change your opinion, but making sure you are aware of which marketing tactics are used helps you evaluate the information more rationally.

2. When you see content that is untrue being spread with marketing tactics, try to point out unproven facts. This may be uncomfortable, but you are more aware of marketing tactics than the person sharing it, and stopping a lie works best the sooner you do it. The longer you allow it to stay unchallenged, the more people share and like it, the more damage it is doing. The responsibility really is yours.

3. When you see a post spreading lies with marketing tactics, check to see if the account is a troll account (see the Trolling and Trolls chapter in this book to see how to do this). If so, report them or block them. That way you will never engage with them again, and trolls love attention. So take that away from them.

4. Hold our policymakers accountable for what they say on the record. Send a message to their office and tell them they represent their entire constituency and you are holding them accountable for not doing so come the next election. An easy way to send a message to your representation is to type the word RESIST and send it to 50409. This is a free ap that will send messaged directly to your representation based on your zip code. You don't even have to know who your representation is, the ap will figure it out for you.

CHAPTER 4

THAT DOESN'T MEME WHAT YOU THINK IT MEMES

4.1 A Post-Literate Society

We are now in the age of post-literate online communication. Don't believe me? Just look at this text conversation between a friend and me. We know exactly what we are talking about and a word isn't said.

4.1 This text conversation only contains Gif images. What do you think this conversation is about?

We now understand implied meanings with only an image or short captions. We understand the nuances of most rhetorical commentary. We are mastering communicating quickly and effectively. Traditionally, reading takes time. It takes time to first read, understand, and sometimes reread and digest information. That is why the meme is so powerful. We see it and almost instantly understand it. The meme is the perfect marketing tactic for today. Memes are the new shared common language

The greatest advantages memes have are also why they are such a problem. They are easy to consume, and you can be bombarded by dozens of them a day. That means we consume dozens of biased messages repeating themselves over and over, reaffirming our biases. It is changing how we are processing ideas and issues because we are internalizing these ideas as our own, when really, they were created by a stranger who doesn't deserve your trust.

Memes have the most impact on those who don't have the tools to discredit the information placed in front of them. Think about people who try to avoid politics, who don't go online that much, older generations who struggle/refuse to learn new technology, or who don't understand common marketing tactics and online nuances. They are the most likely to be influenced by fake online posts using marketing tactics to push political agendas.

I know sometimes we all have to turn off politics for our own sanity. I get it. Some of us aren't generally all that interested in politics. But knowledge is power, and understanding how these memes leverage marketing will help you see the tactics that are swaying your thinking.

In the following sections I am going to share some of the most common memes I see. Most of them rely on faulty logic or tropes that are overused and predictable. I am going to look at them through a marketing lens. Like I said earlier, marketers double down on what works. These all work, and we will keep seeing versions of them going viral until we stop falling for them and stop sharing them.

4.2 Fallacies

Almost all divisive memes are fallacies. And you are not going to recognize that if they align with your own bias(es). When you see a post that is for your side of an issue, your confirmation bias will take over and convince you it is true. If it supports your opinion, it will appear truer to you than anything opposing your beliefs that might cause you to be skeptical.

Fallacy memes use some kind of logic even if the logic used is faulty. You can follow any kind of logic anywhere you want to go. And if you want it to support your side, you will follow it and support it as a completely logical conclusion. Trolls know this, and that is how these suckers are winning.

In this section I am not going to go into all fallacies. I am going to look at common memes from a marketing perspective; many of these leverage marketing tactics that are fallacies. I highly recommend you read *An Illustrated Book of Bad Arguments* by Ali Almossawi if you want to be better informed on the subject. I promise you, the more you educate yourself on fallacies and faulty logic, the less trolls win.

4.3 The False Analogy

Often called a weak analogy, these super common memes go viral around heated topics. These memes make their point by comparing two things that are related in some way, but the severity of the relationships are often proportionally false. They show the impact of one thing having the same magnitude as the impact of the other. But they simply aren't true. The relationships are always twisted and are not a good analogy for the situation.

One key sign that the analogy is going to be wrong is if it compares an inanimate object or animal to a human life. The tricky thing about these analogies is they use some logic that is correct but some that is twisted. And you can follow any kind of logic, even twisted logic, anywhere you want to go. The more biased you are to the subject, the more strongly you will believe it to be true. It will be almost impossible to convince you otherwise, because the way you see it, the logic leads perfectly to the conclusion that makes sense to you.

4.3.1 This meme shared by Donald Trump Jr. was wildly popular with news outlets and is majorly Islamophobic. Beyond that, if you look at it logically it is also a false analogy. Because of anti-Muslim beliefs and the fear associated is so ingrained in his target market, people couldn't even look at it objectively and realize the logic was twisted and didn't actually make sense. See chart 4.3.2 to examine the incorrect magnitude of the impact this meme is claiming.

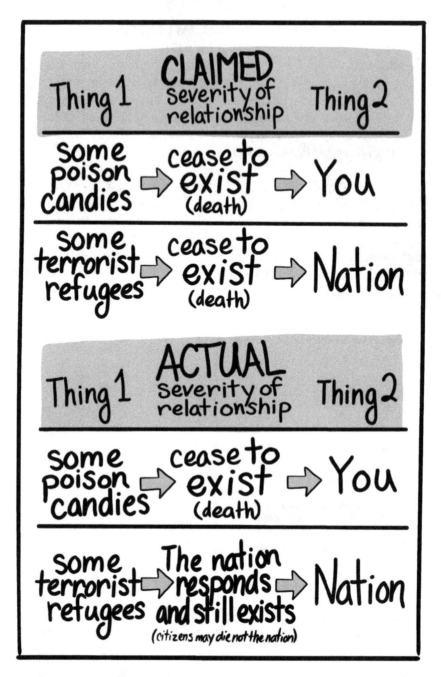

4.3.2 *In order for an analogy to be an accurate representation of circumstances the severity of the relationships between two things compared have to be the same. The exact magnitude of one relationship has to be the exact magnitude of another when being scaled up. His claim is death or ceasing to exist and it just isn't plausible that the most heavily weaponized nation in the world would cease to exist if some terrorists came here. They have come here and the nation still stands. I am not saying a human death wouldn't result from either of these scenarios. I am saying the severity of the comparison is exaggerated and therefore doesn't actually support the point despite being given as evidence of such.*

4.4 The Story Meme

Hypothetical story memes drive me bonkers. They are fairy tales we post as the truth. They follow a stereotype that is anecdotally truthful in certain cultures. If it is our belief, we identify the concept as truth. Even though what someone is hearing or looking at is completely a made-up story, they are still being led where the storyteller wants them to logically end up. And remember, you can follow logic anywhere you want to go.

4.4 This is a portion of a viral made-up story meme that talks about illegal immigration. There are real racial problems as the meme clearly copares a white family to a nonwhite family and conciders the white family to be the one

93

with appropriate behavior. Throughout the entire meme it repeatedly compares two employees with one working illegally. No mention of employers being accountable. This lack of accountability on the employer leans even further into the racial tropes. It wants the white people to be the victims in the story and the people of color to be the only ones doing wrong. If you told this story including the employer breaking the law in their hiring practices the narrative probably wouldn't fall on racial lines. People shared it as if it was a real story. The racist anecdote in their minds was completely true, and the missing information about the employer wasn't part of the story they had accepted as truth.

These stories usually leave out huge chunks of information, which is beneficial to the storyteller's goal. I have had people argue with me up and down that a story about reporters at a bar was basic economics. Don't underestimate these stories. Our brains are programmed for stories, and they are our highest form of communication. It is why religious texts are stories, it is why the greatest songs are stories, and it is why when we tell people about our day/life, we tell it as a story. Stories are marketing.

4.5 The Image with a False Caption

As crazy as it sounds, you can't believe your own eyes when it comes to images with false captions. Calling these miscaptioned or misleading, as many fact-checking websites do is too nice of a descriptor for these kinds of memes. They are lies. They are showing you an image and lying about it, but your instinct is to believe that the evidence you need is right in front of you in the picture. It isn't. It is a lie.

The best example I have ever seen was this image posted by a troll account on the 4th of July. Not only was this timing of marketing completely suspicious, but there's more. The caption claimed the person in the image was parking in a space they weren't supposed to be parking in. Since this falls back on the trope of disrespect and patriotism, hatred spread it like wildfire and people were calling for vigilante justice. But here is the truly scary thing. Parking space signs in parking lots aren't law unless they are spaces for people with disabilities.

4.5 The original post included this person's full license plate, which put their safety at risk. There is no evidence this person was ever confronted, that they are female, or that they are not in fact a Purple Heart recipient because having an indication of service on your plates is not mandatory. We are taking the word of a troll who posted a call for justice on someone being unpatriotic, and timing their marketing to the 4th of July. And when I found this image it had over 16,000 shares and you can see the commenters truly think this person deserves to be taught a lesson over something that can't even be proven. Versions of this post pop-up everywhere to this day with posters reassuring their followers it is true and it should be shared to shame this person.

Now let's think a bit more about this. What if this person is a veteran and even a Purple Heart recipient? There is no law saying you have to have veteran plates on your vehicle if you served. So what if vigilante justice is being brought on a veteran who is actually parking in the space designated for them? How horrible is that?!? How absolutely horrible is it that a troll posted someone's actual license plate on the Internet with a call for justice! All this photo is proof of, is furthering their own agenda and need for attention. If anyone doesn't deserve our trust, it is a troll.

Now let's take it a step further. What if this troll just wanted to get back at their ex-partner and posted their van so people would come after them? What if they are a veteran? What if? Okay, this is a bit extreme, but the point is you don't actually know. There is absolutely nothing verifiable here, but the story is so compelling that we go along for the ride. And the person whose license plate was posted is now searchable and in danger. I have seen this trick used in GoFundMe projects for hurt animals, shaming protests, and more. All of it unverifiable at best and misleading lies for attention at worst. A compelling story and an image that could possibly represent the story is just enough validation for us to not question it.

In anticipation of the hate e-mails I will receive for this section, let me be clear, I am not making a claim that this behavior we are being told is happening is justified. I am stating that there is no actual proof that the caption is truly representing what is going on in this image, despite it appearing to line up. You can't take a troll's word for it when they had so much to gain and used so many marketing tactics to sell this story to you.

4.6 The 'Expert' Perspective

The 'expert' perspective presents a convincing argument why one way of seeing things is the correct way, backed up with 'expertise.' And if this aligns with your beliefs, you will believe their perspective is the right one.

What is so hard about perspective is we all think our perspective is the absolute truth. Rachel Hollis talks about the concept of how we see things as we are, not as they are. She gives the example of the perspective of watching a burning house. To a bystander, that burning house is a sight to see. To a reporter, it is a front-page story. To a firefighter, it is a job to do. To the homeowner, it is their life, security, and memories. And to an arsonist ... well, it is something completely different. And that is because we see things as we are, not as they actually are.

Another huge problem with expert perspective is we aren't listening to the right people for direction. We are assuming if they are an expert of some kind their perspective must be irrefutable truth. But it isn't true. The arsonist is not the person to ask on how to prevent home fires. The firefighter is the person to ask. You wouldn't ask the reporter what you can do to help, you would ask the family. Now, if you want to spread the word about collecting donations for the family, the reporter is the expert to help get the word out.

The 'Expert' with an adjacent field of knowledge

Many of these kinds of experts will talk on YouTube videos or on blogs about their expertise at length and how many years they have spent in their field, but most of the time they still aren't qualified (hence they are giving their misguided two cents from their driver's seat or their kitchen instead of an actual office). They don't have an actual office because they aren't an expert, and what they are saying would make a company liable to a lawsuit.

You see people talking about health, what is in our food, economic structures, and all sorts of other things. But at the end of the day they probably don't work in the actual field they are claiming expert authority about.

The 'Expert' With a Perspective of Vested Interest and Bias

This one can be tricky to spot because the person can really have experience, but that experience probably comes with a huge vested interest and a bias. A great example is a CEO of an oil company talking about climate change. He may be an expert in oil, which impacts the environment, but he probably isn't a climate change expert. Despite having knowledge on the subject, he isn't a climate scientist. He also has an extremely vested interest in taking the side that keeps his company going. He wouldn't be in the business of oil if he truly cared he was ruining the environment.

These kinds of experts come from many strict social groups, such as religious, military, or even industry-specific groups. But you have to understand that they only have one strict view of the topic and are leaving out chunks of information either intentionally or because they themselves have a huge information gap on the subject.

4.7 Truth Videos

Anytime you see a video where someone is about to tell you the truth about an entire group of people or unveil an elaborate conspiracy theory, just remember you really can't batch people together like that and an entire conspiracy theory needs more verification than a video on YouTube where anyone can post content. Sure, that video will really 'stick it to 'em,' but these overgeneralized videos are mean-spirited and far more hateful and harmful than helpful. The way they give opinions is often disguised as fact by the speaker's confidence, perceived authority/ expertise, or storytelling skill. These videos also tap into anecdotal beliefs that have become cultural truths by sheer repetition. They spread like wildfire because hate and fear is easy marketing, even if it pretends to be an enlightened truth. The only truth you need to know is that you just shared a post that hasn't been verified and you backed the huge sweeping generalization that screamed at someone you know. This kind of BS authority should never be confused with the truth.

4.8 A Photoshopped Status and Fake Quotes

Statuses, quotes, and posts by elected officials are extremely easy to fake. It is even easier to believe them now, because things our elected officials actually say are so divisive that we don't think to check if they're real. We find ourselves thinking that this isn't any lower than what the bar is set at, and we don't bother to check.

But I can fake a status in just minutes. It is this easy.

There are even apps now that make fake statuses just to be humorous. This is another example of a place where you need to check the source before you post. Go check the original accounts. Go check the time that it shows it was posted.

This also goes for quotes. You should think of these as facts that need to be checked. If you see a quote attributed to someone and you don't see where the original article is linked, you should suspect it is fake even if it aligns to your beliefs.

4.8.1 This fake photoshopped status went viral after Trump claimed you need an I.D to buy groceries.

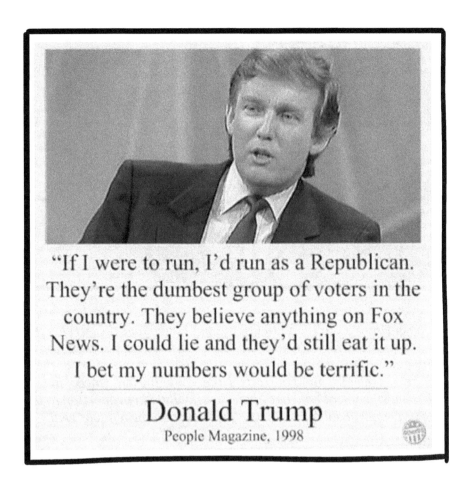

"If I were to run, I'd run as a Republican. They're the dumbest group of voters in the country. They believe anything on Fox News. I could lie and they'd still eat it up. I bet my numbers would be terrific."

Donald Trump
People Magazine, 1998

4.8.2 This quote is not real, yet people shared it like wildfire without giving it a second thought because of all the outlandish things Trump says. It felt real.

4.9 The Photoshopped Image

Anything can be photoshopped. Say it with me: "Anything can be photoshopped." Seriously, it is just so easy. And things are just getting worse. Video manipulation and faked video is going to become more and more common, so you have to check if images are real.

A great way to check if an image is real is to go to a desktop computer and use reverse image search on Google. Go to images.google.com and upload the image or the link to the image in the search bar by clicking on the little camera icon. Does this image appear on any news sites you have actually heard of? If not, you most likely have a manipulated image on your hands. Check the Fake News chapter to learn more about identifying news sources online.

4.9 The image of Hillary Clinton with Osama bin Laden was an extremely popular image spread before the 2016 election. But it was just a photoshopped image. This version of the meme shows the side-by-side comparison of the original image on the right and how it was altered on the left. Once you see the original it is almost comical how badly the head is done in proportion to the real photo. But people absolutely believed the image on the left was real.

4.10 Memes Made to Scare You

So many memes are created just to scare you into an opinion. Honestly, most of them are so horrific I refuse to share them in this book. They include genocide, images of killing, and worse. This one is a perfect example—a picture of a child who isn't even a real child! It is a digital drawing of a child and I can't find any linking information for the image. Seriously, if a meme is scaring you, remember that it is a marketing tactic. They want to control your opinion through your emotions.

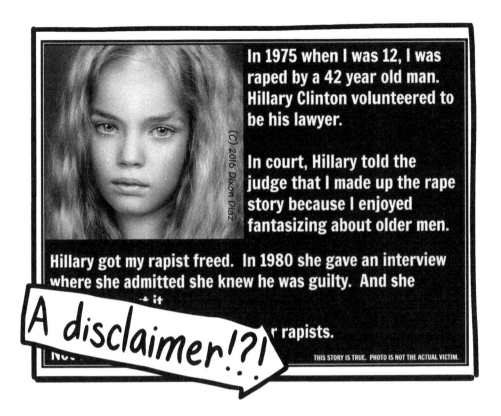

In 1975 when I was 12, I was raped by a 42 year old man. Hillary Clinton volunteered to be his lawyer.

In court, Hillary told the judge that I made up the rape story because I enjoyed fantasizing about older men.

Hillary got my rapist freed. In 1980 she gave an interview where she admitted she knew he was guilty. And she ... it

r rapists.

THIS STORY IS TRUE. PHOTO IS NOT THE ACTUAL VICTIM.

A disclaimer!?!

4.10 This is one of the weirdest viral memes I have ever come across. The meme has no links backing the claims and the really strange thing is the image isn't even a real photo. It is a digital drawing of a made-up girl! And even more bizarrely the meme has a disclaimer in the right corner saying the story is true. Those words aren't evidence of anything. It has got to be one of the craziest uses of scare tactics I have ever seen that worked wonderfully. I lost count of how many people I knew that posted this.

4.11 Facts and Numbers are Hard

Did I mention people suck at numbers? Yeah, they do. There are three very specific ways in which people suck at them when it comes to memes that have facts or numbers used.

The Facts and Numbers have no linked information

These tend to be an image with no linked information backing the claim in the image. But it can also be a video, or even a caption to an image that claims some kind of fact. If you can't prove a fact, you have to throw it out. It is your responsibility to validate the information you share with your friends and family.

Hillary Targets Family Farms!

Triple Taxation!
Targets Farmers/Small Business

- Proposes death tax at 65%
- This proposal will take farms from families
- The large family farm is worth more than most realize due to the land value.
- Even if the family is barely making it they are land rich and dollar poor at times.

✳A 65% death tax forces the sale of the property.
✳This is theft!

This is posted on her website as her tax plan, it is the top tax bracket in the plan. Check out her tax plan, she's the one that posted it and is all smiles about how she is going to rob the rich. The problem is the rich protect their wealth with an army of accountants and lawyers. Family farms are heavily affected as are small businesses. Most don't see them being that valulable but they are, and the ones that pay the fee are not the guy that worked for it, and already paid taxes on it, it is the kids that want to keep doing what their parents did and can't because the government forces them to sell. Large family farms like the ones in the midwest are the ones that are hurt most and then end up in the hands of corporations.

If I had know this would go viral when I posted it I would have provided more information then. Sorry for that. I pulled the information off her twitter feed when she posted her plan a few days ago. I made the meme.

THINK ABOUT THIS, IN THE 70'S TONS OF BIG RANCHES AND FARMS ENDED UP IN THE HANDS OF CORPORATIONS. NOW the liberals are after the crop producing farms. DO YOU REALLY WANT THE BIG CORPORATIONS AND GOVERNMENT IN CONTROL OF ALL THE FOOD?

It was posted here!

Or maybe it was here...

4.11.1 This meme has no links to the information it is claiming to present. Even more hilarious is the caption claims to have pulled the information from her website and then later on says it was pulled from her Twitter. Which one did you get it from? They then tell you to go read it because they know you won't. All without any links because they know you won't go check yourself.

Facts and Numbers Sound Real

Memes with facts and numbers trick people into sharing them mainly because they sound like they could be real. They seem possible if not completely valid because they align with our bias and we have probably even heard the same made-up facts quoted by divisive political commentators or politicians. This isn't an accident. Remember, repetition is a marketing tactic and the best marketing tactics double down on what works. And if a lie claiming to be fact is repeated enough, it becomes anecdotally true in culture no matter how many times real numbers rebuke the claim.

4.11.2 These numbers may sound real to me and close to what I have heard time and time again. But without links I have to throw them out and not assume this information is true.

Not Understanding the Context of the Facts and Numbers

Seriously, people are just REALLY bad at numbers and the critical thinking skills that are needed for context. I have seen more people post facts, numbers, or infographics representing their side of something, but they actually shared information that was against their stance or was out of context. Remember, you can follow logic wherever you want to go, and the trolls who post this kind of content want you to see it their way. They want you to completely ignore the bigger picture. These appear to have authority because the chart or numbers look irrefutable. It takes critical thinking to realize what the information actually means in the bigger picture, and there are a ton of ways to present information that makes your case the way you want others to see it.

4.11.3 One of the easiest ways to claim victory is to take credit for something you didn't do. This Tweet and the responding Tweet criticism showcases how the numbers being boasted by the AZ Republican Party weren't all because of Trump. When you factor in the context of the actual timeline of him being in office as President, the majority of growth happened under Obama.

4.12 Saint vs. Sinner

The Saint vs. Sinner meme has many iterations. But usually it is just painting your side as a saint and the other side as the sinner. It is completely hypocritical and forgives your side of any and all wrongdoing; however, this meme has some far more dubious forms that include classism and racism and we need to look at those too.

Classic Saint vs. Sinner

Have you seen memes that lob accusations at someone and then forgives another of all sins? Odds are they have no links to information, and they are completely biased. By turning a blind eye to what people on your side are doing you are not holding them accountable to the same level to which you are holding your adversaries.

4.12.1 This meme turned out to be almost too poor-quality resolution for this book, it is blurry and hard to read but it is such a clear-cut example I am still using it. What matters is you can clearly see the partisan bias is a perfect example of Saint vs. Sinner marketing. One side is forgiven of all due to partisan bias and the other is being held accountable to higher standards.

Racist Version of Saint vs. Sinner

Unfortunately, these are all too common. And when you point out the racial bias in them, people basically try to explain how this issue is 'different.' But it isn't. This is racism. If you show a stereotypical picture of someone of color behaving badly and show them in contrast to someone who is white who is behaving a way you approve of (typically it is a white male who has served his country), you are being racist. These types of racist tropes were used all throughout history and during times of slavery. It isn't something new and this issue isn't 'different.'

4.12.2 You can justify a meme about an issue any way you want. But if your post is clearly divided by race using stereotypes that highlight 'white in the right' then you posted a racist meme.

They Don't Deserve Better Because ... Saint vs. Sinner

A classic tactic of division is to pin lower classes against each other, so they don't unify against the upper class. We see it all the time. My income is far closer to someone making minimum wage than the multimillionaire advocating that his company can't afford a minimum wage increase. But as long as I focus my energy on those making minimum wage not deserving better, the power stays firmly in the hands of the multimillionaire. If you have read *The Art of War* by Sun Tzu, you know this is basically a strategy of divide and conquer.

4.12.3 Whenever you see the shaming of someone's occupation as not being good enough for a living wage by being pitted against another occupation, know it is a marketing tactic. No one is in the wrong for wanting a living wage and no one trains for higher paying jobs hoping they will be used as a reason to keep someone else in poverty. Also, do you think someone got these people's permission to make them a viral meme?

Another common example of this is the idea that others don't deserve better because those in the military deserve better. It stages helping one group over another as a mutually exclusive concept. It works really well at stopping people from asking for more by shaming their worth. I can't imagine anyone signing up to serve their country hoping they will be in a meme used to shame their fellow citizens out of having better lives. The point of serving your country is to make people's lives better, not to be used as leverage to keep others down.

WE GET PAID LESS THAN MINIMUM WAGE

AND YOU'RE DEMANDING 15 BUCKS AN HOUR
TO SLAP A BURGER ON A BUN

4.12.4 I really do wonder if these men were asked if they could be turned into a meme to promote the position of holding down our county's minimum wage? If you don't know the answer to that question, then don't share these. If they didn't give their permission, think of how disrespectful sharing this image actually is.

4.13 Playing Switzerland

"We must always take sides. Neutrality helps the oppressor, never the victim. Silence encourages the tormentor, never the tormented."

\- Elie Wiesel

We often place ourselves in a position of not being involved in an issue because it is comfortable. This can show up as being Switzerland and wanting no part of it or claiming both sides are horrible. But both stances are a form of self-defense through inaction. These two stances are basically different sides of the same coin. Sometimes these memes claim we should all get along no matter what our political beliefs. Sometimes they try to claim neutrality in politics by saying each side is equally bad. These memes are designed to try to appease everyone because they don't hold anyone to a level of accountability they deserve. Whether people who share these memes realize it or not, they are basically being complicit to bad things happening, because they come off as reassuring both sides they are right. This is all done in hopes that everyone will like them by posting this meme that doesn't take sides.

4.13 This meme makes you complicit by abdicating your responsibility to learn the facts and add informed commentary all in the hopes of being likeable. Bonus points to you if you noticed the spelling error in this one too.

4.14 Cause vs. Cause Shaming Meme

The hardest part about these types of memes is they are completely subjective. You can yell at someone that your cause is more important than theirs and they can turn around and say the exact same thing to you. If you have trouble with this, try comparing two non-politically charged causes. Would you tell someone they shouldn't support prostate cancer research because breast cancer research is more important? No, you wouldn't. We should always celebrate people caring enough to put in the effort to make the world a better place even if the effort isn't subjectively the one we deem to be most important.

When Notre Dame was burning, the world's media covered every moment of it and billionaires rushed to restore it. Right now the Amazon is burning, the lungs of our planet. It has been burning for 3 weeks now. No media coverage. No billionaires. #PrayforAmazonia

4.14 Comparing two causes is always going to be subjective as to which one is priority. Shaming one cause with another is a very effective marketing tactic.

4.15 Apples vs. Oranges

This is a meme that is used to compare two different things as an attempt to shame one side. This is very similar to cause shaming; however this tactic usually hinges on a lie. It claims the two circumstances are exactly the same and one side is behaving inappropriately but in reality, it is comparing two different things. The lie holds up based on the knowledge that people will not question the information placed in front of them because the photo looks to be enough evidence. You can think of this as an elaborate form of an image with a false caption.

4.15 This image is not comparing the same medals. Obama is bestowing the Presidential Medal of Freedom which is the highest medal that can be given to a civilian. Trump is bestowing the Medal of Honor which is for military. With different purposes for these medals you are witnessing a comparison that is Apples vs. Oranges marketing.

4.16 The Mutually Exclusive Myth

Mutually exclusive myths are embedded in our culture and are usually a form of cause shaming. They usually compare two issues that are somehow related and subjectively claim that you are focusing on the wrong one. This false dilemma is used to shame people taking action on an issue you disapprove of. When it comes to causes, it isn't one or the other. You can almost always do both. But this zero-sum mindset is so embedded in us by politicians and belief systems that people can't think of problems in any other context. There is almost never a time that you can't disprove these memes by simply reminding yourself that we can do both.

4.16 There is no reason to compare these two problems as if one has effect on the other. The image shared below fixes the top image from a mutually exclusive myth to the question that really needs to be answered.

4.17 The Highlight Reel

I touched on this before as a marketing tactic, but it is important to understand that this marketing tactic is a super common type of meme. It shows up in two ways:

The Side By Side Highlight Reel

This kind of highlight reel is put together to show someone doing a type of behavior repetitively or in a contradictory manner. It can be used to show hypocrisy more than anything. But take them with a grain of salt. Context is important. If the clips are out of context this can still be a huge form of propaganda. Even tweets and short statements need to be looked at in the context of the whole statement.

2.11 Donald Trump has become notoriously known for changing his stances on political topics based on personal benefit or party affiliation. Sam Morrison, photographer and artist in Los Angeles has even created a business off of it. He created flip flops that feature side by side tweets of Trump's changed opinion.

The Fear-Based Highlight Reel

This one chops up what people say into snippets without context and often ties it in with headlines, misdirection, and terrifying images of war and genocide/mass murder. The only logic to all of it is making you fearful. I have seen so many people get riled up and share these pieces of propaganda as evidence. It is terrifying for me to see people believe so whole-heartedly in these videos and I can't imagine the fear it must have instilled in them to take it as gospel.

Many of these fear-based highlight reels rely on conspiracy theories and target that very specific and vulnerable audience. That is why they are so effective even though all the negative imagery is unrelated and doesn't actually make any sense.

4.18 Callout Culture Posts

With a camera in everyone's hands at all times, bad behavior is just a button away from being uploaded onto the Internet for all to see and pass judgment on. And you might be surprised to learn that I am not completely against callout culture posts! I know you didn't see that one coming, did you? I am all for the exposure of people's bad behavior that they thought was secret. But as with everything, there is a catch.

Sometimes I don't think we are helping. Sometimes I think we are just gossiping or worse, we don't know the whole story. While we are busy patting ourselves on the back for putting this person on blast, we might really just be gossiping and not helping at all. Callout culture can also take a bad turn when personal information is shared, such as a home address, phone number, and other identifiable information. That's never okay. This shared information can put someone in danger. I have even seen people put someone on blast and they misidentified the person! How terrifying! Be sure you aren't just showcasing to people how petty you truly are, because if you put someone on blast publicly, how do you think people assume you act in private?

4.18 A young man's contact info was spread around the Internet for a disrespectful confrontation with a Native American elder. No matter how you feel about the confrontation, the problem was, it wasn't the right person's contact info.

4.19 Insult Memes

"When haters go after your looks and differences, it means they have nowhere left to go."

- Greta Thunberg

No one will take your side if you insult them. But seriously. Name calling, insults, and any kind of bullying are for the weak-minded. These spread like wildfire because they make us laugh and they really stick it to the other guy! But it is just a form of verbal abuse.

I have even been targeted myself with a particular bullying meme shared by people in my life I love and trust. I took part in the Women's March and afterwards many of my loved ones shared a meme calling the protesters fat. Commenting on a woman's appearance is a double standard that is really never used to tear down men. The Women's March took place specifically to call out how women in politics are treated differently than men. This sexist insult critiquing our jean size instead of our political beliefs basically reaffirmed how women active in politics are treated differently than men. This was not lost on me even if it was lost on those who shared it.

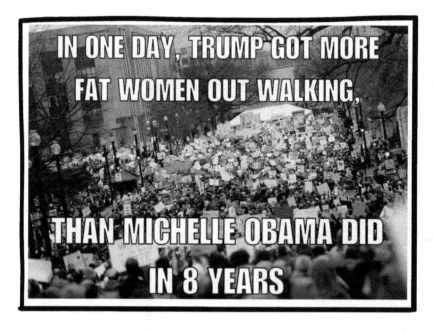

IN ONE DAY, TRUMP GOT MORE FAT WOMEN OUT WALKING, THAN MICHELLE OBAMA DID IN 8 YEARS

4.19 If you go after someone by being a bully it shows your immaturity and your inability to be able to give a constructive argument. This was one of the most popular memes I saw in my feed shared by my friends and loved ones after the Women's March.

4.20 Nuance is Key

"Knowledge sometimes is not facts, it's context."
- Diane von Furstenberg

Often the nuance is lost on how a meme might be perceived by someone having an opposing viewpoint. The way a meme is worded can have a completely different context than how you read it to someone on the other side of the issue. It often lies in the phrasing. The social proof of a meme shared many times makes us believe that it is a good thing to say. Take this meme for example:

4.20 This meme was originally a post by someone on Facebook made public for everyone to share. It was making a commentary about children separated at the border by the timing of when it was made and using the word 'separated.' It immediately went viral.

A friend of mine shared this meme and I wrote her, warning that it should probably be taken down. She disagreed with me and said it was how she felt and kept it up. People started yelling at her in comments on the post and in messages and she ended up in tears. She then took the post down and wrote another one apologizing. She told me that a family member of hers was in the service and he hadn't seen his kids in over a year. She thought she was saying how much the situation at the southern border reminded her of her family's and all these children without parents made her so sad. She didn't realize the nuance of this meme. It said to many who read it that those other children at the border weren't as worthy as the children of men in service to their country. And arguably that is how it is supposed to read.

The saddest part of this whole experience is that her actual thoughts were beautiful and caring. If she would have just posted her thoughts to begin with, the debacle wouldn't have happened. We see these memes so many people have shared that we think it is social proof that it is a good idea to share them. We think that somehow a stranger's words are more bulletproof than our own and we share in confidence because so many others have done the same.

But why would you trust a stranger's thoughts over your own? They are most likely posting something hurtful on purpose. These types of memes spread extremely fast, because not only do many people share them without truly understanding the nuances in the political climate of what is being said, but they also get even more engagement from people who perceive them as the insult they were intended to be.

4.21 The Long Reposted Passive Aggressive Status

We have all seen these snarky self-righteous diatribes on political topics spread by person after person in our feed. These usually shame others for their behaviors, and they act a lot like a classic chain letter. What they all have in common is reassurance to repost because of the social proof given by so many other people sharing it. The problem is these posts usually have all kinds of tropes hidden subtly in the content. They usually contain shaming, types of bullying, racist content, and sometimes they are lies pushing a certain agenda. These posts are always extremely divisive and very pointed. You know exactly who you are targeting when you post them.

Also, keep in mind that by posting these you make your profile easily searchable to anyone, (think hackers and bots) because of the weird distinct phrasing in them. Those distinct phrases make you an easy target if your profile isn't set up with adequate privacy setting. I myself used this reverse searching of exact phrases to find who I knew posted these for my book. It is that easy to do.

4.22 Batching Memes

These memes rely on extreme examples to generalize an entire group. They tend to take extreme actions of some and assume that these actions of the extreme can predict other actions of an entire demographic about another related topic. Millennial or Boomer bashing, anyone?

I even have my own assumptions that are a form of batching. Whenever I find out people are hunters, I typically assume they are against gun control and want to arm teachers, but that just isn't the case. Many hunters want reasonable gun control, so I shouldn't just batch them into a stereotypical belief just because of another belief they have.

4.22 This meme showcases an example of batching people into multiple opinions by assuming one opinion or affiliation assures they believe the other.

4.23 Political Cartoons and Political Art

I am always going to have far more respect for someone who creates a political work of art or cartoon than someone who creates a meme. It takes skill and real dedication to learn and perfect an art form. People spend their entire lives becoming better artists, and I highly respect that. Artists tend to see the world in different ways than most people and this can be impacted by their tendency to have nontraditional social circles and life experiences. Throughout history artists have shown us different perspectives on issues and have made us feel empathy and discomfort in a way that many other forms of communication in this world simply can't.

But be aware that political art and cartoons can also be problematic memes or tropes. Political cartoons and political art can be as divisive as any meme out there. If you see one that you find to be problematic, you should hold it to the same standards you hold any meme you see on the Internet.

4.24 Patting Myself on the Back Meme

Of all the memes out there, these memes rely the most on habit. In *The Power of Habit: Why We Do What We Do in Life and Business,* by Charles Duhigg, a habit is described as a Cue, followed by an Activity, followed by a Reward. People share them without even thinking. It is ingrained in their social media habits to do so. I am looking at you boomers because I constantly see people of older generations share these.

These memes typically show someone our society would hold in high esteem and ask you to 'like' or 'share' the post to support them. More often than not it is a white male who served our country in the military, but it can be religious in nature or anything we consider ourselves a good person for spreading.

4.24 This image of Dr. Joe Medicine Crow was turned into a meme for troll accounts to get more shares by guilting those who saw it into believing they were doing the right thing by getting this image more likes and shares. In reality all it did was give troll accounts a boost. I doubt Dr. Joe Medicine Crow gave his permission for this to be created and would probably find sharing this meme pretty disrespectful if he ever saw it.

It seems by sharing these, you are supporting the people in the meme, right? Well you aren't, you are basically patting yourself on the back for being a good person and that is about all. It is a habit. When you see these, you instantly think you should share, people will appreciate it, and that makes you feel really good about yourself. It happens in an instant. This is classic **Cue** (seeing the post), **Activity** (sharing the post), and **Reward** (getting likes and feeling good about yourself). There are actually some really harmful concerns to think about with these memes and I am going to touch on two of the biggest.

The first problem with these memes is where they originally came from. Most of them come from troll accounts that help them get discovered by more people. The virality of these feel-good posts help trolls get more shares on their divisive content later. If one post from an account goes viral algorithms push more of that account's content out thinking they are posting important content. So when you share these, be sure they are not from troll accounts. If you still want to share the meme once you find out it comes from a troll account, then save the image to your phone or computer and share from there. You shouldn't share their original post because you are helping them spread division and hatred later.

The next problem is that you don't know if these people ever wanted to be a meme. Do they even know some stranger on the Internet made them into a meme? Did anyone ask their permission to turn them into a meme? Do you think they want their faces spread across the Internet so the people sharing it can feel better about themselves based on how many 'likes' or 'shares' they get? Probably not. If someone did that to me, I would be so embarrassed. Wouldn't you? And if someone doesn't know they are being shared around the Internet—or worse—didn't want to be shared around the Internet, then what you are doing isn't supportive. It is patting yourself on the back at the expense of someone you hold in high esteem but are actively disrespecting. If you can't verify that the person in the photo wanted to be shared around the Internet like this, you are most likely violating the privacy of a private citizen and making them an Internet spectacle to feel good about yourself.

4.25 Patting Myself on the Back
Trojan Horse Meme

Like all memes that have you patting yourself on the back for being an amazing example of the human species, these memes completely rely on your belief that sharing them proves you are putting good out into the world or even helping people. You either believe you are doing a public service by sharing it, taking a stand by sharing it, or are sharing feel good information with others. I have noticed that a large majority of these twist real information into Trojan horses for their true agenda.

People want to feel good about what they are spreading so they spread really fast without anyone questioning if what they are sharing is real. Their sinister nature can actually be racist, a slam against a group of people, or pandering to cultural tropes.

The divisive message in the content is the real reason it was made. It is to reinforce stereotypes, hate, and a planned agenda. It just adds to the repetition of division when all you thought you were doing is sharing something anyone else would share.

General Eisenhower Warned Us.

It is a matter of history that when the Supreme Commander of the Allied Forces, General Dwight Eisenhower, found the victims of the death camps he ordered all possible photographs to be taken, and for the German people from surrounding villages to be ushered through the camps and even made to bury the dead. He did this because he said in words to this effect: 'Get it all on record now - get the films - get the witnesses - because somewhere down the road of history some bastard will get up and say that this never happened' This week, the UK debated whether to remove.

The Holocaust from its school curriculum because it 'offends' the Muslim population which claims it never occurred. It is not removed as yet. However, this is a frightening portent of the fear that is gripping the world and how easily each country is giving into it. It is now more than 60 years after the Second World War in Europe ended. This e-mail is being sent as a memorial chain, in memory of the, six million Jews, 20 million Russians, 10 million Christians, and 1,900 Catholic priests Who were 'murdered, raped, burned, starved, beaten, experimented on and humiliated' while many in the world looked the other way!

Now, more than ever, with Iran , among others, claiming the Holocaust to be 'a myth,' it is imperative to make sure the world never forgets.

4.25 The entire purpose of this meme is to stoke hatred towards Muslims by creating a bogus story that people feel a responsibility to share. When people share it, they feel they are raising awareness to an important issue but really, they are spreading Islamophobia.

4.26 Slacktivism

> *"We can talk about making a difference, we can make a difference, or we can do both."*
> — Debbie Millman

Now just to be clear, spreading awareness is not slacktivism. Sharing articles about a cause, raising funds for something, or showing up in person and sharing that experience online is not slacking. For this type of post the focus is on showing your support for a cause online and doing nothing else. Slacktivism falls into the realm of self-congratulatory posts, showing solidarity, or support for something that is publicly displayed online but has no action behind the sentiment based on your actual ability to help. It comes off as disingenuous. Because if you really cared, wouldn't you have done something?

I am going to pick on the most controversial and obvious form of slacktivism. Yep, you guessed it—posting a sentiment of "thoughts and prayers" for a tragedy. As I discussed previously, we all think our religion is the right one, and that will never change. Growing up Catholic, I can tell you that thoughts and prayers did not make saints, it was their actions and impact that elevated them to sainthood.

> *"There is something deeply hypocritical about praying for a problem you are unwilling to resolve."*
> — Mirosolv Volf

Online posted sentiments ring hollow to many in the face of a tragedy such as a mass shooting. And even if you truly believe you are calling on your divine creator to help and consider prayer an action, you are abdicating any of your own personal responsibility to impact the systems that are in place in our society to create change. This duality comes off as completely hypocritical. Isn't the issue you're posting about also worthy enough for you to call your representatives and ask them to do something about it?

If you think about it in a nonpolitical way, if someone I know wants to be a better parent, they not only pray about it, but they devote time, research, and action to make it happen. And that is why slacktivism is so frustrating. It is because we know more could be done by so many and instead all they do is post a culturally appropriate response and move on.

4.26 Every time a tragedy happens people share images on social media in support. Although showing solidarity is a beautiful sentiment it falls short of taking an action that can actually create change.

It is even worse when someone of real ability to make change responds with nothing but slacktivism. They often address how a cause is so meaningful to them in a well-worded tweet but then never bring about the change we know they are capable of enacting. Personally I (and many others) look at these types of responses as pandering—appeasing the social construct of what you should say, but never taking real responsibility.

> *"I used to believe that prayer changes things, but now I know that prayer changes us and we change things."*
>
> - Mother Teresa

4.27 Memes with multiple tactics

Some of the most viral memes use multiple marketing tactics to make you spread them quickly. Sorry to say but conservative memes really are the best at using multiple tactics. On the pages that follow I am going to show you just a few examples of viral memes and posts that leveraged multiple tactics. You get bonus points if you can see marketing tactics I don't mention.

If you're genuinely concerned about saving the lives of children, then focus your energy on banning processed foods instead of banning guns. They are 28 times more likely to die from obesity than be murdered by a firearm.

4.27.1 This meme leverages cause vs. cause shaming marketing, and it also claims a statistic without a link to prove the number is true. The number marketed may sound true but without a link to the information it has to be thrown out. I personally wouldn't share it because it is voyeuristic and shows a child who doesn't deserve to have us share them as an example of our own personal opinions.

This one was everywhere

"In the end I believe my generation will surprise everyone. We already know that both political parties are playing both sides from the middle and we'll elect a true outsider when we fully mature. I wouldn't be surprised if it's not a business tycoon who can't be bought and who does what's right for the people. Someone like Donald Trump as crazy as that sounds."

~Kurt Cobain. 1993

4.27.2 This meme leverages the marketing tactics of nostalgia, authority, and a false quote lying about the image it represents. Because so many people respected Kurt Cobain for being an innovator, he has authority even in death, and his legacy is being used to spread something he never said. It also had social proof because it was everywhere.

4.27.3 This viral post is Long Reposted Passive Aggressive Status, a Patting Myself on the Back Trojan Horse Meme, and markets all of it with an image with a false caption that leans on respect and patriotism. That is a ton of marketing tactics! And look how many shares just this one image got – over 600,000! The whole purpose of this post is to sew distrust in media by claiming they aren't showing real news. It leans on patriotism and honor to make you feel absolute disgust that the news didn't share this and pride for what the news supposedly hid. Shame on them!

So many people shared it with pride because it obviously needed to be shared. Here's the thing, the caption written is not truth. The photo was taken after the Warrior 100K Ride not a private event held for Wounded Warriors 10 weekends a year. That is why the news isn't covering these supposed 10 weekends a year, it is because those 10 weekends a year is a lie.

Donald J. Trump ✔
@realDonaldTrump

Our case against lyin', cheatin', liddle' Adam "Shifty" Schiff, Cryin' Chuck Schumer, Nervous Nancy Pelosi, their leader, dumb as a rock AOC, & the entire Radical Left, Do Nothing Democrat Party, starts today at 10:00 A.M. on @FoxNews, @OANN or Fake News @CNN or Fake News MSDNC!

8:37 AM · Jan 25, 2020 · Twitter for iPhone

30K Retweets   **117.2K** Likes

4.27.4 This is a standard example of a tweet made by Donald Trump. It has authority because of who he is. It feels authentic as if he said it. It has name calling, bullying, it discredits news by calling it fake, and is very retweetable because it really sticks it to 'em! So much marketing in less than 240 characters!

4.27.5 *This meme is a Patting Myself on the Back Trojan Horse Meme that uses apples to oranges marketing to spread Islamophobia by leveraging patriotism. Did you get all that? This meme has been around a long time, but I saw a few people I know post it in 2020 folks. It just blows my mind that something like this is even still spreading.*

First of all, it is just five different pictures in five different places. So who really cares what is in the background? Comparing different places is ridiculous and is an Apples to Oranges comparison. Also, it leverages a made-up term of a 'Muslim Prayer Curtain,' which isn't a real thing but if you are too scared to educate yourself it sounds real enough. And lastly it took me just seconds on Google to find that yellow curtain in photos or our President all the way back to Reagan and it still exists today with Obama's successor also in front of it.

4.27.6 *Presidents Ronald Reagan all the way through Donald Trump in front of a gold curtain used to spread Islamophobia when marketed as a replacement for the American flag and unpatriotic.*

125

4.27.7 This meme leverages facts with no links, the numbers sound real, so no one checks despite the lack of links meaning they have to be thrown out. It also has a giant helping of cause vs. cause shaming and leverages victimhood. You should feel really sorry for all those poor gun owners that still have their guns. Just seeing this meme makes me want to facepalm.

4.28 What Are the Best Practices for Sharing Memes?

Before you share a meme, ask yourself if it is truly what you stand for? Ask yourself if it is an oversimplification of your words? If the meme is an oversimplification of your words, you should write your actual words. Don't let an image made by a stranger speak for you.

You can share absolutely any meme you want. If the meme is something you want to share, I highly recommend saving the image to your phone or computer first and then posting it. This way you can be sure you won't be spreading the reach of any troll accounts. If you read Chapter 6 on Trolls and Trolling, I help you to identify if it is a troll account you are sharing the information from. But to be safe,

I would save any image first so that you don't support something you don't want to support. Sometimes trolls post feel-good posts to get us to share their content and help them reach more people. Those feel-good posts getting high engagement tell computer algorithms to show more of their content to more people. It tells the algorithm these accounts post important information so all of the troll's posts now get seen by more people. Don't give the trolls any help.

If the post you want to share is a video, I recommend doing a thorough check of the content. Is the account a troll account? Is it offensive and heavily biased? Does it claim facts without backing them up? Since you typically cannot save videos before posting, you should try to be highly diligent before you share the content and give it your stamp of approval to your friends and loved ones. If there is one thing fishy about that video, don't share it. Guilty until proven innocent.

Do your research. Yep, just make the effort to see if what you are sharing is real. Try to prove it is wrong instead of looking for shreds of possiblity to confirm your own bias. It isn't hard. You are online at the very time you are about to share something, and you know what else is online? Google. Google is also online, so stop being lazy and use it.

Another great way to spot bogus memes is to learn about false logic and bad arguments. For a quick and humorous read on bad arguments I again recommend *An Illustrated Book of Bad Arguments* by Ali Almossawi. Because once you learn what to look for in a false argument it is almost painful how you will be able to recognize them everywhere.

CHAPTER 5

FAKE NEWS

5.1 What is Fake News?

> *"The phrase 'fake news'... is being used by autocrats to silence reporters, undermine political opponents, stave off media scrutiny, and mislead citizens."*
>
> - John McCain, former US Senator

Fake news can be two things. Fake news is either someone calling a story they don't like fake news to discredit the story, or it is actual bogus news.

Let's get one thing straight right now. Calling something fake news because you don't agree with it is NOT acceptable behavior. People in high positions of authority do this all the time and dismissing facts and discrediting journalism as a whole works really well for them. Many have trained their followers to embed this phrase in their everyday political conversations to discredit real legitimate news sources. If you practice this, you need to start being better at articulating what you are talking about instead of perpetuating the use of this phrase.

Now that we have an understanding, let's talk about actual fake news. Fake news stories are used by people in power to divide us and to cast further doubt on situations and to turn lies into anecdotal truths. Most people don't know the difference between propaganda and a real source. I have had people share scary troll content with me, conspiracy theories, sketchy websites, and more, trying to convince me that these sources were legitimate evidence for their opinion. We need to have a talk about all of these things.

5.2 Always Guilty Before Proven Innocent

This section is so important I am writing it twice. Always, always, always assume that what you see online isn't true until you build a case otherwise. This is the opposite of court cases. The burden of proof is on you to prove the content is innocent, and it is guilty of being fake news until you do so. Why? Because it is your reputation on the line. If you can't prove something is real, why would you then share it?

Each of the following sections is going to list the criteria for proving that content is real, and here's the thing—they are all interconnected. If a meme references an article on a blog as a source, the entire article should be deemed true. If even one aspect of content seems fishy, you throw it all out. Everything builds on one another. The sins of one aren't forgiven because you think another is legitimate.

5.3 Memes aren't Evidence of Anything

You should NEVER consider a meme as a source of news, ever. A meme is not news. It is not truth. It is an image with words on it. That is it. I have had people be absolutely insistent that a meme was evidence for their cause.

I can tell you the truth about memes right now. You will never solve an issue with a meme. You will never blow an issue wide open with a meme. And you certainly didn't find irrefutable evidence that no one has considered before 'hiding' on the Internet in the form of a meme. When detectives try to solve a case, they don't scroll through memes to do research.

So how do you tell if it is true? You have to find evidence that it is real. This requires it to be linked to legitimate articles supporting exactly what it says. You don't get to share a meme and then try to find something to back it up in hindsight. Sometimes articles have memes connected to their post and it makes your job easier. But even those articles need to be proven true to back your source.

And if you still share memes with a bogus marketing tactic after the previous chapter then ... have I taught you nothing?!?!?

5.4 How to Tell if a Website is Bogus

Always assume a website is bogus and biased until you do more digging. The easiest way to throw out the content on a website is if you have never heard of this site before 2016. Tons of fake websites popped up around the 2016 election with the sole purpose of pumping out divisive content. I own www.generalmediaassociation.org and that sounds legit. But it isn't a source for information more than just this book. Names like 5DailyNews.com, LeftLiberationUnited.org, OurConservativeCaller. com, TheAmericanLiberationAssociation.org, the IndependentIntelligencer.com, and NBC.newsnow.com are all names I just made up (and they could exist in the future), but a believable name isn't enough. You have actually had to have heard of the source before 2016.

But there are exceptions to every rule. I follow articles by a news source called News & Guts. Why? Because it is run by Dan Rather. I trust Dan Rather. And even though it doesn't sound official, I know it's a reliable source. If you actually know who runs a site and you trust them, it is probably a good source of information.

Also, make sure the website you are referencing is up to date and has legitimate sources. Content will usually tell you when it was published. I have had people send me websites that were last updated in 2002 as a source. Yeah, no. A site that has been inactive for years isn't a source.

5.5 How to Tell If an Article You Shared is Biased

The biggest sign that an article is total bullshit is name calling. If your article uses name calling outside of quoting people, it is biased bullshit and is most likely an opinion article, not fact. It is easy as that. That will rule out 99% of fake news or biased articles. These articles can't help themselves. Having integrity in journalism is something they don't care about, and the name calling makes it completely evident.

My favorite trick to tell if an article is biased bullshit is to check if the exact same information is on other fake news sites. If you Google an exact phrase from the article you are reading (the more outlandish the better) and it shows up on a ton of news sites you have never heard of, it is fake news. Why? Because fake news sites are lazy and they just copy and paste what other fake news sites post. In classic marketing style they just take the easiest route and publish what works.

And don't forget that if the article is from a website you haven't heard of prior to 2016, you should throw it out.

5.6 Blogs and YouTube Channels As Sources

Blogs, vlogs, or YouTube videos are not sources unless they are publishing first-hand experiences. Do you understand what I am saying? I am saying that the person posting has to show you the experince and not just their opinion about it. They had to actually attend the protest they are talking about, or bake that cake to perfection right in front of your eyes. Even if it looks extremely professional and has a huge following, they are still an independent source operating by their own rules and have not been varified by journalistic standards.

I don't care if they are a full-time reporter and blog on the side. There is a reason why they can't write that content for the news sources they work for. I don't care what medical credentials they claim to have. Never take medical advice, political advice, or financial advice from a blog or YouTube any more seriously than an opinion from a stranger. If they had real credibility, they would be writing in medical journals, for mainstream news sources, or on a platform that needs more professional varification than unboxing videos. A quick check on the credibility of these is to Google the title. If it comes up over and over on sites you have never heard of-throw it out. Fake news sites will repost viral content and don't care about varifyng the information. Going viral on sketchy sites guarentees it is bs.

5.7 Fact Checking Websites

If you find that the content you are looking at is referenced as false on a fact-checking website, you have to throw it out. You won't find everything that is fake on these sites but finding false information on one of these sites means you have to throw it out immediately. Websites like FactCheck.org, PolitiFact, Snopes, Washington Post Fact Checker, and NPR Fact Checker are great places to look for false information. I often Google a phrase or headline from a story + the words 'fact check' to see what comes up.

But here is the thing—there is so much fake biased crap on the Internet these fact checking sites can't even keep up. They can barely keep up with the daily false tweets from the Trump administration. Use the other tools I gave you first to judge for yourself, because these sites can't possibly have everything.

Sometimes the information you find is so biased that you have a huge information gap about a topic. Googling the term 'media bias chart' will show you a chart of how biased media news sites are, and it is a great place to figure out how to judge the credibility of the news site you are reading. Then read about the topic from a site with the opposite viewpoint and form your own conclusion.

5.8 Mainstream News Sources Aren't Fake News

Mainstream news sources have gotten a bad rap because of politicians calling stories they don't like 'fake news.' But ask yourself, why wasn't the mainstream news considered 'fake news' before the 2016 election season? It is because planting the idea of distrust in the media into the mainstream was a targeted marketing tactic. This distrust allows misinformation to thrive. Politicians have said the words 'fake news' over and over so many times that we now believe it to be true.

Free press is a fundamental watchdog of our democracy. I don't know about you but watchdogs bark at anything driving into the yard. I am the one that has the responsibility to check out what is going on based on them notifying me. When they do their part I still have to do mine. The reason 'fake news' has stuck is because news moves fast, is ever changing, and is created by humans and isn't infallible. Current politicians are using marketing tactics to create distraction marketing. I know so many people that can reference 'that one time' a news anchor got it wrong, but completely forget about the 50+ times they personally shared a fake conspiracy on Facebook and claimed it was proof for their opinion.

Just like any other bullying technique, the term 'fake news' has stuck on mainstream media because it touches on a point of truth. There are truly tons of fake news articles out there and there is always a chance that mainstream news is going to be wrong or the story will evolve over time. But I would take one wrong story in a week by professionals any day than a conspiracy theory filmed in some guy's basement.

Also, think about how you hear about news sources being wrong. Politicians and shady news sources scream it from the rooftops, creating a false-positive that it happens all the time. It doesn't. It is a story of one being blown up to represent the entire profession.

5.9 Why Do Conspiracy News Sites Sometimes Break Big Stories?

Imagine I have basketball season tickets and I know that every half-time they choose ten season ticket holders for a chance to win $10,000 by making a half-court shot. Every single week I practice that shot. I am actually getting pretty good at it and have put in hours of time single-mindedly hoping my name gets called to try to make that shot. Towards the end of the season, my name gets called and I nail that shot! The crowd goes wild! People can't believe how amazing at basketball I am and how talented I truly am!

But am I? Am I truly talented?

The answer is yes *and* no. I am talented at making that half-court shot. I have worked single mindedly to be great at it. Could I hold my own with the players? No. Absolutely not. I might know a great deal about the game since I attend all the games, but I am not a professional. But I nailed that one thing because my entire focus went to that one thing. It is the same concept with conspiracy theory sites. They spend all their time trying to prove other news is wrong. That is what they do. When they make that shot, they look absolutely amazing. But they are not the professionals. They have just focused all their time discrediting other news sources. Real news sources have the entire game to worry about. They do not spend their time on the singular act of discrediting other news sources, and they are the professionals and have a job to do.

5.10 Clickbait Headline

Unfortunately you can't blame news publications for having clickbait headlines, or judge their credibility based on the headline alone. It is marketing. So as long as we keep clicking those headlines, they will keep making them. Fake news, real news, and satire all rely on income from ads based on you reading stories and sharing them.

The article stands on its own merit and should be judged using all the other factors pointed out in this chapter. Think about it this way—if you are uncomfortable with how far the headline spun what the story was about, then throw it out as a source, but don't let a headline you dislike speak for the content of that article or an entire publication. You reevaluate. Every. Single. Time.

5.11 Satire

I love satirical articles and websites. The humor and the scary realization that they are almost too true is fodder I eat up! But as I said, they are almost too true. More and more I am finding that people cannot tell the difference between satire articles and real ones and it is actually a real problem. As our leaders become more and more outrageous, the line between reality and satire has helped perpetuate stereotypes and lies to epic proportions. Elected officials have even regurgitated satire and conspiracy theories as fact. All of this is desensitizing us.

When sharing satire online I suggest you actually tell people it is satire. It is the responsible thing to do. And if you are unsure if an article is satire, the best thing to do is to Google "is [name of publication] satire?" You will usually find your answer pretty quickly.

5.12 Best Practices for Identifying Fake News

1. Memes aren't evidence of anything. If any meme claims a fact in image or caption without a link to information-throw it out.

2. You have had to actually heard of the website before 2016 to consider it a reliable source. Always check the web address to make sure it doesn't just sound real, looks like it is real, must be real because it looks professional and has millions of followers. If you havent heard of this source-throw it out.

3. A website referenced should always be up to date. A website that hasn't been active for years is not evidence of anything.

4. If you are posting an article or meme that has facts from other sources, all of those sources should be linked and you should check them to make sure the sources follow all above rules.

5. Blogs and YouTube are only good sources if they are first-hand accounts.

6. If an article uses name calling outside of quoting someone, it is probably bias bullshit.

7. Check on Google for any outrageous phrases from the article. If it

only pulls up other sites with names you have never heard of consider it fake news.

8. Google media bias chart and try to find articles with the opposite bias about the same topic to double check your sources.

9. If you find the information proven false on any fact-checking website like FactCheck.org, PolitiFact, Snopes, Washington Post Fact Checker, and NPR Fact Checker-throw it out.

10. If you aren't sure-THROW IT OUT! Consider it false unless you can prove otherwise.

CHAPTER 6

TROLLS AND TROLLING

6.1 Trolls

The Internet troll is a well-known concept and almost every single person has felt the sting of a hateful trolling comment online. But it has become increasingly apparent that people have no idea how to spot a troll, how to stop obsessively sharing their content, or how to identify trolling behavior in others and in themselves. Trolls and trolling behavior are so prevalent in everyday content I see shared that they get their own chapter. And maybe for once this is a kind of attention they don't want. We are going to talk about impact, why they do what they do, various types of trolls and trolling behavior, and how to recognize their accounts and content.

6.2 Why Do Trolls Do... What They Do?

The answer is simple. Because we give them attention. They wouldn't post that type of content online if they didn't get a response. And they use classic marketing tactics and almost every example of posts I have shown in this book to elicit a response. Political content is one of the easiest and laziest ways for trolls to get people to give them attention. It is almost guaranteed to get people to stack onto their content. It can quickly go viral and the talking points are basically created by the world at large. There is no need to have an original thought. Just jump on the bandwagon of what angers people the most.

Trolls are trying to feel significant in a world where there is so much noise. They want to be heard above the rest and these tactics garner attention. It often shows up in bullying and other abusive online behavior in their quest to feel important.

You need to understand that trolls post content they hope will go viral based on their target market's predictable opinion and response on a topic. They are targeting you and you are responding as predicted. And honestly most of that predictable behavior is not you showing up at your best. Even if the original account looks like it has a purpose that you support, you should know they would change the account tomorrow if you would stop feeding their need for attention. They are not crusaders for a cause, they are crusaders for a click and attention.

6.3 Trolls Go After Their Target Market

Troll accounts are very selective on who they are for. This makes it easier to get you to spread their content. They are specifically oriented toward certain target markets, such as conservatives, gun lovers, sports team enthusiasts, liberals. More specifically, they target people from different lifestyles like southern pride, Latinx culture, or even racists. They keep their messages very on target and are sure to only spread hate about those outside the group, so the intentions are harder to see by the members. A single idea of hate is much easier to spread far and wide than an actual diverse range of thoughts and opinions on any subject.

6.4 Trolls Thrive in the Information Gap

Trolls thrive in the information gap. They have an innate sense of what information their target market isn't aware of or doesn't care to know about, and they exploit that to its fullest potential. They create scenarios, generalizations, and flat out dangerous lies knowing their base doesn't know information is missing. The knowledge that their target markets don't know, or won't bother checking, means the lies they share will spread like wildfire.

Take the bathroom bills for an example. These bills tried to limit bathroom use by assigned birth gender. Troll accounts were accusing transgender individuals of being sexual predators without any actual evidence of this being the case. Troll accounts across the Internet completely swapped the idea of a sexual predator for that of gender identity because the information gap around gender identity was so large with their target market. They knew their target market didn't know the difference between the words sexualize, sexual predator, sexual orientation, sexual identity, and transgender. They knew they could swap out the meaning and people would be horror-struck over something they would never do research on.

The information gap was HUGE. They then focused on fear and it worked. They spread so much misinformation that you almost couldn't have a real conversation about the topic. In reality, a person is considered transgender if they identify as a gender they weren't assigned at birth. It in no way means they are a threat or a sexual predator.

Take for example a conversation I had with a friend online about the subject. This friend was in strong support of these bills after seeing meme after meme on the subject. I tried to explain that this law was discriminating against a select group to keep them out of public spaces, very similar to segregation. And in response all I would hear is some version of, "I do not want a sick-o pervert raping my child." Trolls had filled the information gap with fear and hateful rhetoric, which made rational conversation almost impossible.

My friend was parroting what they had seen online and because content posted by trolls was all they had seen; their information gap was filled with hateful misunderstandings and dangerous assumptions. Finally, I shared a picture of a bearded gentleman and asked my friend what bathroom he should be in. They responded that this individual should be in the men's restroom. I agreed, pointing out that under the bathroom bill this gentleman would be sharing the restroom with their little girl because he was actually born a she. It wasn't until that moment that my friend finally understood what was going on and how this bill actually put people in high-risk situations.

James Parker Sheffield
@JayShef

@PatMcCroryNC It's now the law for me to share a restroom with your wife. #HB2 #trans #NorthCarolina #shameonNC

10:37 PM · Mar 23, 2016 · Twitter for iPhone

6.4.1 This transgender man shows just how ridiculous the bathroom bills are by tweeting an image of himself. If he were to follow the new law he would put himself in dangerous and inappropriate situations and thus to follow the law he can't go anywhere and use a public restroom. But if your information gap is filled with fear about the situation it will be really hard for you to recognize actual situations over made up hypothetical ones without blatant examples like this.

Most often you see the information gap filled by trolls right after or during a controversial event. The danger is that it spreads so fast that real information doesn't have a chance. Many people on the other side of the information gap don't even know they should be helping to clarify the situation. Because the information is targeted, if you aren't in the target market, you don't know it even exists until the damage is done.

6.4.2 Trolls love the attention they can get when you don't have enough information to understand a situation. They can spread as much crap as they want based on fear. It gets them tons of attention and helps them get great reach online.

6.5 How to Spot a Troll

Walks like a duck, quacks like a duck—it is a duck. What you have to understand is that trolling is a type of behavior and that behavior can make anyone a troll. Heck you could even be a troll! Or a relative of yours could be a troll. And there are all kinds of ways to spot them. But the number one way to spot a troll is to simply look at what they post. Look at their pictures. Is it all divisive memes? Are all their comments accusatory and divisive? Then they are a troll. End of story. Trolls won't pull these things down either because they love getting the likes and shares on them.

6.5 Trolls can support any issue or demographic. But the easiest way to spot them is to look at what they post. Everything they post will be divisive crap. Their photos or media they post is an easy place to check for this.

But honestly, take a look at what you post. Are you a troll? Is your uncle Albert a troll? Is your mom a troll? Ok, but maybe your mom is sharing memes from another account and that account is really the troll account right? Well, sort of. There are amateur troll accounts, policymaker trolls, professional trolls, affinity group trolls, and more types we will cover in this section. If you or someone you love posts nothing but divisive content, then the verdict is clear ... they are a troll.

6.6 Professional Trolls

Professional trolls are people who get paid to be controversial. They can host talk shows, they appear on the news, write books, give speeches, and they also write opinion articles. They commonly use tactics that revolve around conspiracy theories, name calling, bullying, blaming minority groups for large issues, and have an absolute expert level of denying any responsibility for what they said or implied. They create content on a more professional level than other trolls. Their videos are usually well produced, and they have the financial and professional means to get millions of views. Amateur troll accounts share this content constantly because it looks credible and easily spreads with social proof.

What is so horrible about these accounts is they create the controversies for money. The more outlandish they are, the more attention they get which leads to better ratings and they make more money. Everything they say is basically a strongly held opinion just said with confidence and professional level media tactics, which gives them authority. They create their own logic about issues and then take it anywhere they want to go, as long as it blames other people. And because people have seen them in professional capacities, the masses take what they say as fact.

They are protected under free speech just like we are, and they know exactly how far they can push that line before they get sued. When pressed about taking responsibility for the content they put out, they often describe what they do as mere entertainment. They don't take responsibility for shifting entire political party opinions and entire populations of target markets on political matters or for putting others in danger due to the false information they spread.

Professional trolls are also experts at leveraging victimhood. They also act like victims so much so that these type of radio programs are often called 'victim radio.' They blame problems on everyone else and constantly reassure their target markets that they are the victims. These tactics work incredibly well at solidifying their conspiracy theories because when we feel like the victim or feel wronged, we look for someone to blame. Many have crossed lines that have gotten them assaulted in public and even held accountable legally. When their hatred comes back at them in confrontations or when people hold them accountable for their actions, they cry about being a victim of mistreatment. They completely rely on the false ideal that freedom of speech means freedom of consequences.

They do put in a ton more work than your typical troll, but at the end of the day they are just putting hate out into the world. That isn't an accomplishment to be proud of, despite being done professionally and being financially lucrative.

6.7 Policymaker Trolls

Despite what recent politics might have you believe, when someone is elected or appointed to represent a constituency, they represent that entire constituency, not just the people who give them funding or are in their same political party. Let me say that again. When someone is elected or appointed to represent a constituency, they represent that entire constituency, not just the people who give them funding or are in their same political party. This is why they are called public servants. They serve the entire public they represent.

When you are a policymaking public servant, everything you post online is on the record. Everything you say can be scrutinized because you are speaking for every person you represent without exception. The higher up you are, the more people you are speaking for. This is why policymaker trolls cause such a stir. When they use name calling, when they threaten people, when they use derogatory statements towards groups of people, when they say hateful things at rallies and cause an entire crowd to stack up hate against others, they are betraying people in their constituency and are encouraging a select group of followers to stack on to hatred on the record. These actions alone are enough to understand why our country is so divided.

Great leaders don't tear others down to build themselves up. They speak with humility and the understanding of the gravity of every word that comes out of their mouths, and how their words will be taken as authority by those who perceive them in a position of power they must abide by.

By bullying or threatening those they are supposed to be serving, a large constituency doesn't just feel betrayed, they can watch it happen on a live video feed or take a screenshot of the words now in public record. Why wouldn't people become hostile towards a leader who has now thrown them under the bus or worse, threatened them?

But this is actually brilliant from a marketing standpoint. Their target market latches onto the ideas coming from authority and moves the messages forward. They internalize the hatred as their own beliefs. When you are in the policymaker's target market, this behavior will be hard to see, and you won't perceive the words as being that bad since they aren't directed towards you. You may think what is being said is deserved. You might even feel camaraderie because people bond over mutual hatred of others. But this behavior is absolutely not normal.

Think of it this way. If you are a parent, what you say in front of your children matters, and you are accountable for every word they hear coming out of your mouth. Would you lie to them about what is going on right in front of them to confuse them? Would you praise one child and make fun of the other publicly? Would you tell groups of people to boo the child that isn't your favorite? Of course you wouldn't. That isn't treating all your children with the respect they deserve or taking responsibility as their parent to lead by example. Make the scenario about a boss and his employees, or a mayor and his townspeople, and the behavior is still not okay. However, this is how you get ratings, how you get coverage on every website, and how you get all the attention a troll could ever want. We need to do better and hold policymakers accountable.

6.8 Trolls as Nonprofit Groups

One thing I find the saddest about so many troll accounts is that they pretend to be supportive of certain causes or claim to be mission-based, but in reality, 99.9% of what they do tears others down and elicits mob-like mentality responses. That is troll behavior. The accounts can claim to support family values, patriotism, limited government, or even different faiths. But just like other troll accounts, they spend all their time creating division and going after people they have defined as targets.

Think about it—real nonprofits or charities don't have time to spread hate because they are working to do good, right? It is just that simple. Some of these just have social media profiles and some of them have real websites and are really registered as nonprofit organizations. A great resource to help identify trolls as nonprofits is the Southern Poverty Law Center. They list hate groups on their site that disguise themselves as nonprofits.

6.9 Amateur Troll Accounts and Affinity Groups

Amateur troll accounts and affinity groups are the ones that make content go viral. The amount of time they spend posting and spreading misinformation and hate is incalculable. They are the foot soldiers and the amount of time they dedicate to spreading misinformation is exhausting.

The amount of content they generate on a regular basis is terrifying. There are thousands, maybe millions of these accounts, and they push out millions of divisive posts every single day. I actually don't know how they have so much time on their hands? They not only create their own content. but they repost and share the content from all the different types of troll accounts such as professional troll accounts, and policymaker troll accounts.

What makes these accounts harder to spot is often they have names that sound like a regular person. Or the affinity groups will appear to be focused on pride about where you live, pride in your country, your favorite cause, or your favorite sports team. By appearing to be accounts without malicious intent they are able to trick their target market into interacting with all their content. When you look at the account, the majority of what you see is divisive content. They stoke fires and add controversial and hateful comments to articles to create division. They use the idea of stacking hatred everywhere they go to speed up division that possibly wouldn't even start without them planting the seed. Their main purpose online is to stoke arguments. Even if they post a few things you might agree with and might not find hateful, their true agenda is to get you to interact with all their content and by gaining your trust they are all but guaranteeing you will spread the divisive content too.

6.10 Bots, Russian Accounts (and other countries), and Fake Websites

Bots are accounts that are controlled in mass by computer algorithms that either take information from a real account to create a profile, or they just leave their profile fairly empty. Sometimes the names are things that are patriotic, but also their names can sound completely normal. A great way to spot a bot is to see if they have had an account earlier than 2015. Most of these accounts popped-up after that as they started to influence the 2016 election. If you check their account, all you will see is divisive content. And they repost and repost and repost in algorithms with one another.

The Russian accounts are harder to spot because they can engage in conversations. Like bots, the accounts tend to be no older than 2015 and have varying levels of information in their profiles. Their accounts mainly focus on divisive topics, causing people to rally around extreme opinions. Their original content can often have grammatical mistakes and if you check their account you will see only divisive content just like any other troll account. The Russian accounts also tend to be on the far left or far right of situations, creating chaos. They will post from the far right cheering on racism and other ideals that are extreme. But they also have accounts on the far left that threaten people and are catalysts to pretend movements. They create a false positive of the number of extremists out there. In doing so they pull the conversations to more extremes than it would take without them. Their entire goal is to get us to stack onto things and escalate division.

Fake websites are used by bots, Russians, and trolls to share content that resembles real articles. It is a great way to diversify their content and to fool people into believing a lie is real. A great example of an article from bogus websites I constantly see shared is an article about some celebrity loving your tiny hometown. These are almost never real, and they still get shared like wildfire by everyone and their neighbor.

This is not a conspiracy theory. This has actually happened and as quickly as platforms can fight them, they change and evolve and try new tactics.

6.11 Celebrities and Trolling

A group I constantly see trolled online is celebrities. People are constantly throwing hate at them for sharing their opinions on politics. People for some reason feel celebrities owe them something or should 'stay in their lane' when it comes to politics. But celebrities are private citizens despite being public figures. They may have high visibility and high influence, but they are in no way responsible to any constituency the way a policymaker is. A celebrity may be in the public eye, but they are not a public servant; in fact, they are only responsible for their own careers, family, and their own beliefs, just like we are as fellow private citizens.

When you think about it, celebrities actually put their financial stability at risk by being political. We have seen story after story of a celebrity posting something online and losing their job or their fans for it. But remember, we are all 100% responsible for what we post online, including celebrities. They are just not accountable to any of us in the same way as a public servant/elected official despite high visibility and influence.

6.11.1 Many conservatives were far more upset at celebrities saying they would move to Canada if Trump won than at the barrage of lies Trump says. This meme is a classic Saint vs. Sinner meme by holding some accountable and forgiving all from the other.

So why do people get angrier at celebrities than politicians? Probably from a misplaced understanding of influence vs. responsibility. Also, remember—repetition is mistaken for liking something. We see a celebrity over and over again in our favorite TV show, and we have misplaced fondness for them. Many people also think celebrities owe them something because of their vast wealth coming from consumers. But in a capitalist society, celebrities are simply being compensated at the market value for the services they are providing. Being entertained by singing, acting, creativity, comedic ability, or athletic ability is highly prized in our society. They are getting paid according to market value of their talent and the amount of revenue they bring in for their employers.

This issue is extremely complex. Politicians point outrage at celebrities as an easy win. Some think a celebrity shouldn't be political when on the clock or want them to be more accountable for their influence. The actual job of comedians is to push the first amendment and people get outraged when they do. Also, there are celebrities serving on boards and in public service positions, so they are both influential and accountable for a constituency. But if your outrage at the 'Hollywood Elite' is higher than your outrage at one of your own representatives, you need to reevaluate why, and think about who actually deserves to be held accountable based on the positions and responsibilities they have.

Mayim Bialik, best know for Blossom and the Big Bang Theory, has a great video "Celebrities & Politics || Mayim Bialik" on Youtube where she talks about having the right to be interested in politics and political issues. I highly suggest you hear what she has to say.

6.1.2 Many celebrities have political opinions just like any other private citizen. When we dismiss them as Hollywood Elite, we are being completely hypocritical since our President is best known for being a TV personality.

6.12 The Impact of Trolls

But why does trolling even matter? It matters because this information is shared over and over at such a rate that it becomes part of public discourse and our anecdotal truth. Trolls are actively pumping out divisive content everywhere. Just one fake meme matters. Just one. Just one can reach and impact millions of people, reaffirming their own bias, and trolls make it a point to put effort into spreading so many that you see dozens every time you go online. And repetition grows fondness. They do such a great job at getting this stuff in front of us that it has changed elections and public opinion. Actual political decisions about people's lives have been made, our elected officials and media outlets are using wording and memes to spread biased ideologies, people have been threatened and harmed, it has fueled hate crimes, and people have committed suicide and killed others, fueled by trolling. It is time to stop feeding the trolls.

6.13 How Can You Combat Trolls?

1. Remember, the easiest way to identify a troll account is by what they post. If they have post after post, that is divisive—you have found a troll. I don't care if you know them. Walks like a duck, quacks like a duck—they are a duck.

2. Look at the affinity groups you like online and the pages you follow. If they look like troll accounts, unfollow them. If you feel like making a bit more effort, report the account and/or block them.

3. Unfollow and/or block any professional troll accounts you may follow and don't tune into them on the television or on the radio. Entertain yourself with something else less toxic.

4. Always check to see if content you want to share comes from a troll account. If so, don't share it. Even if it is a feel-good post. By sharing their content, you are giving them exposure to get more of their divisive content seen. When you share their content, you are telling social media algorithms that their content is important to people. This prompts the algorithms to now push even more of their posts out to more people. You are giving fuel to their next divisive post. "That Uplifting Tweet You Just Shared? A Russian Troll Sent It" is a wonderful article on this topic published by *Rolling Stone*.

5. If you just have to post what a troll posted, don't share their original post. Save the picture to your device and post it yourself. Do not share their content directly. Don't help the trolls if you can help it.

CHAPTER 7

ONLINE PROTEST AND MOVEMENTS

7.1 Protests Gain Momentum Online

When the top three largest protests in US history have happened in less than three years, you know a ton of people's voices aren't being represented by our current government. Protests tend to happen as a response to injustices that aren't addressed by policy, religion, or current culture. Policy and religious texts will never move as fast as societal values. They simply can't. Every single day the words in these texts are put to the test with unforeseen scenarios. That is why democracy, freedom of speech, and protests are so important. Once we know better, many people call on our collective society to do better.

When you think about protests and political movements online from a marketing perspective, there are two classic ways to look at how marketing comes into play. The first is the bell curve with early adaptors, the masses and the late/reluctant adaptors. Some people get onboard with new ideas right away and as the shift happens it eventually brings everyone along. With any new ideas marketed to the masses, this is how the shift tends to happen.

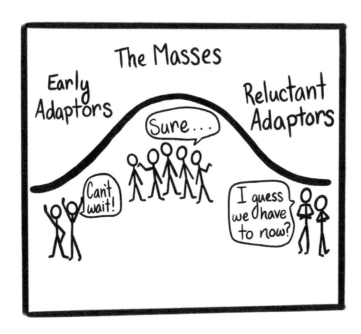

7.1.1 Marketing an idea usually takes the form of a bell curve. First a few people adapt than a larger mass movement joins in and finally holdouts are forced to change.

You can also look at marketing tactics online in a second way as a staircase with different levels of marketing to create the desired change. Changing cultural values happens naturally over time, but sometimes those who aren't affected by injustice don't think change is needed because the issue doesn't affect their lives.

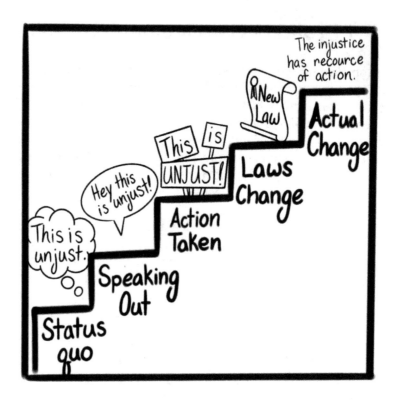

7.1.2 It takes many steps just so people can have the legal ability to change something that is happening that is unjust. Each step takes more and more marketing to move people towards change.

Now consider the slower process of getting policy and religious texts that many people hold sacred changed. Many claim changing them is akin to blasphemy and against the natural order of the universe, and you can see why people dig in their heels and come up with every excuse possible to refuse to change. They also feel personally attacked because their definition of the world is now being challenged. But as we have seen time and time again, policies can change, religious beliefs can change, and people do change.

People regularly tell me that the current protests and online movements don't matter. But throughout history we have seen that protests and movements do bring change. Protests have made huge changes in our country. I think of the Boston tea party, women's suffrage, the civil rights movement, and gay marriage, just to name a few. Tt doesn't matter how the movement spreads, online is just the latest form of rallying the masses.

Movements like the #MeToo movement have catalyzed women to start reporting their assailants, and more serial predators like Larry Nasser will come to justice. We see more women in office than ever after the recent Women's March. Online videos have made us aware of police brutality and the racial discrepancy in their actions. And the Parkland students have caused more movement on common sense gun control policy than ever before, and none of it would have happened with the speed it has without the online components.

7.2 Why Intentionally Starting Small Matters

Many political movements have started online with just a hashtag or small request. I often see them being criticized for tackling issues in a way that has no real impact. But it is really hard to get people to change. But if you train people to make small steps, the big steps don't seem so impossible.

Take for an example the #stopsucking hashtags to ban straws and one-time-use plastics in restaurants. This movement has been repeatedly criticized for focusing on something small. Why ban straws when we still have plastic bottles? Why are the people behind this only focusing on a fraction of the problem? The reason is the marketing tactic of starting small. Their goal is to ban all single use plastic, but our society is so dependent on it and the disruption would impact so many people that by starting small, they are proving it can be done piece by piece.

> *Two of the most powerful words you can hear someone say are me too.*
>
> - Rob Bell

The #MeToo movement has also been criticized for this. How can a hashtag change anything? Well, it did change things... people were overwhelmed by how many people had these kinds of experiences. The millions of stories with the #MeToo hashtag showed that the problem was bigger than imagined. It has called out some very powerful men and has given power to the victims in a way that has never been seen before. Don't be confused by something starting small. Marketing has always relied on the KISS concept and sometimes a simple hashtag and telling your story can lead to real change in the world.

7.3 A Personal Story
Is Truer Than An Assumption

When someone tells you their personal experience, that is a true story. This should be taken as truth about what happened over assumptions or any story you see on the news. Yet I have had times when people I know have said phrases to me such as, "Protesters need to get a job," or "All protesters are paid." On multiple occasions some version of these ideologies has been said to me by people who are fully aware I attend protests without pay and that I have never been on unemployment.

These stereotypical tropes are so fully ingrained in some peoples' heads that it is anecdotally true, and they cannot accept that they aren't. When I remind them that I am neither unemployed nor paid to protest, the usual response is, "Well I don't mean people like you." I can tell you right now a personal story is always going to be truer than an assumption. The marches I was at were made up of real people like me, not assumptions about them.

We do everyone a disservice if we ignore personal stories that don't align with our preconceived narrative. There is a wonderful TED talk about the dangers of the one story that aligns with our beliefs that you should checkout. It is an amazing reminder that the narrative of our biases can be deceiving. Chimamanda Ngozi Adichie's TED Talk, "The danger of a single story" reminds us all that a single narrative or stereotype of a demographic of people isn't the truth. Far from it.

To this day, only one person has actually asked me why I marched. The comment was liked by more than a dozen of my friends who were also curious. They could not understand that I was marching for equality. But I am still so grateful for that question. This person may not have understood why I was there, but they didn't make assumptions. Yes, I was carrying a poster explaining why I attended. But when fear starts to fill the information gap, it is hard to see things for what they really are.

7.3 This is me protesting with my friends at the Women's March. I carried a sign about equality and equal pay because that issue is very important to me. I created all three posters; the artwork of Tess McGill from the movie "Working Girl" was created by my friend and amazingly talented illustrator IBTrav Artworks.

7.4 Miscommunication and the Information Gap Around Protests

Are you making up your own narrative? This is something you have to ask yourself before you criticize someone for their beliefs when they protest. I am liberal and I have marched in the Women's March and the March for Our Lives, and I expected pushback for doing this. I expected to be called unpatriotic, un-American, against our country, an attention seeker, and uneducated on the subject matter, but what actually happened blew me away. There was a HUGE information gap between those who attended and those who didn't. A majority of those who didn't attend didn't even know what the marches were about outside of what trolls told them they were about.

Before you shame a protest, you should know what is in their permit and in their mission. If you educate yourself, you will know when you see this fake news content and know better than to share it. If you are going to discredit a movement, at least do it with real information instead of relying on propaganda that isn't true.

After the Women's March I was blown away by how many hundreds of thousands of people shared a viral post with pictures talking about the disgraceful mess they left behind. The photos did not provide the context that a large march like that actually has cleanup in their permit and that is expected. They also didn't take into account that many signs were left en mass in front of the White House to make a visual political statement of how many people were angry.

I also realized after the March for Our Lives that most people opposed to the march hadn't even read the manifesto and what the protesters were asking for. I can't tell you how many times I heard someone say, "They are going to take all our guns," and "Taking our guns isn't the answer, we need mental healthcare." If any of these people had read the manifesto, they would know that it did not propose taking away all guns, and it called for the ability to do research into gun-related violence and to address the issue as a mental health issue. Instead, these unfounded accusations were voiced over and over discrediting the mission of the movement. The information gap was filled with this rhetoric and that was all it needed for our nation to justify doing nothing yet again.

Many who attend protests don't help the information gap situation. Funny signs with sayings like, "SUPER-CALLOUS-FRAGILE-RACIST-SEXIST-NOT MY POTUS" (a spin on a classic *Mary Poppins* song) may be humorous, but they don't help others who aren't in attendance understand what is going on when they see the coverage. Also, signs that come off as mad or threatening are less than helpful for others who don't actually understand what is going on. The onus of communicating our purpose in a protest falls on those pushing for change. Making signs with parroting statements, inside jokes, or threatening undertones only makes outsiders feel even more disconnected and reassured that the protest is unfounded.

7.5 There Will Never Be the Perfect Victim or A Perfect Way to Protest

"I would rather offer the world my imperfect attempts at positivity than your perfectly articulated negativity."

- Rachel Hollis

I constantly see people arguing that protesters aren't doing it the "right way." But sometimes this highlights that people are more uncomfortable with a particular method of protest than the injustice someone is protesting against. They are focusing on the 'how' not the 'why.' Martin Luther King Jr. went to prison twenty-nine times[7.5.1], and we all know he was truly standing up to injustice despite whether people or the law agreed with his tactics. If you looked at his arrest record you could say he was far from what you would expect from a Pastor. Yet he was doing it all in support of the right thing. The laws were saying he was doing it the wrong way, but history remembers his reason why.

Going against injustice will never be clean and easy. It will usually be messy, because the injustice has been buried in society for so long that there is often not a clear direction or even simple explanations to fully explain what needs to change. Think about it this way: the term 'sexual harassment' was created in 1975. Do you think sexual harassment didn't exist before 1975? Of course it did! But it had been covered up for such a long time with shame and societal protocol that people didn't even know what to call it[7.5.2]. When you are making noise about something no one else has dared to before it is going to be messy and imperfect. It is going to make many people uncomfortable and your every action and your character will be scrutinized. And the easiest way they will have to criticize your cause is to criticize your tactics and your character/past history because that is the most obvious way to shut down a bigger discussion that makes people uncomfortable.

Every single situation is different and has its own nuances. There is no doubt about that. But it has become startlingly clear that more criticism of tactics and character is being applied to people of color, the LGBTQ+ community, and women as justification to dismiss their causes. The criticisms claim not to be related to race, gender, or sexuality, but isn't it interesting how they seem to increasingly apply to these demographics? Would a white male go through the same scrutiny? No, and typically when a white male is criticized people lash out at the possibility of you ruining his reputation over it.

Before you rip a movement apart based on tactics and whether or not those protesting deserve to be heard, by your standards, find out what they want. Is it something you would want? You might just realize you actually agree with them.

7.6 Competitive Victimhood

This concept was out of my reach for a long time, until I read, *The Opposite of Hate*, by Sally Kohn. Now that I know what is happening, I see it everywhere in the current political climate. Competitive victimhood shows up when a movement tries to hold a majority group accountable for their actions. That group being asked for accountability will then claim they are the real victims in the situation. Tthis goes back and forth with each side stacking on to the next thing claiming to be the bigger victim. It doesn't matter what our side did, we swear the other side did something worse. It doesn't matter how badly someone has suffered; we are now suffering more. The victimhood stacks on and when you feel you are being victimized that is how hate grows. This trend of competitive victimhood is embedded in the discourse and marketing we see around protests and people countering them.

Competitive victimhood is rampant on both sides of the political spectrum, but the best example is in the NFL. Player Colin Kaepernick sat during the national anthem to protest police violence against African Americans. He then consulted with a veteran and found out that kneeling was more respectful to veterans, but he kept up the peaceful protest. Soon it caught on. *And people were pissed!!!* It didn't matter that the kneeling was done in consultation with a veteran; half of our country felt completely disrespected and collectively agreed veterans were disrespected. They were now the victims, and so were veterans.

There of course is a great deal of nuance in what happened, but the current administration leveraged victimhood as a marketing tactic, and everyone just stacked on. It was amazing and terrifying to watch as history repeated itself. The gross outrage from people online over this peaceful protest was animalistic. The competitive victimhood was reminiscent of white people screaming at the Little Rock Nine, who enrolled in the all-white Central High School in Little Rock, Arkansas, in 1957. The white students and families were not victims in this situation, but they claimed to be. And their belief in their own victimhood justified their reactions.

But looking back, I can tell you it was the most amazing marketing I have ever seen around victimhood. Our Vice President even flew out to a football game purposefully to leave when the kneeling protest began, just to fan the flames. Victimhood was leveraged everywhere. Again, Trevor Noah does an amazing job explaining the leveraging of victimhood in an episode of *Between the Scenes*. The information is in the resources section of this book.

7.7 Cause Shaming

"Shame corrodes the very part of us that believes we are capable of change."

- Brene Brown

Shame is used against people fighting for a cause because it works. Shame is one of the most powerful tools we have culturally to change a person's behavior. Cause shaming typically involves a comparison of the protest or movement with another cause, with a subjective claim that it isn't worth fighting for. It could also infer that it's shameful to ask for change in the first place. Saying that people are either in the wrong or ungrateful for what they already have shames a movement from both those perspectives.

We talked about the cause vs. cause shaming memes in this book but it is important to understand that cause shaming goes wider than just memes. These ideas spread to the mainstream and end up in talking points everywhere from the White House to news articles. And it is important to understand the tactic being leveraged as extremely effective marketing. There is actually no reason to cause shame if the cause is making the world better. You can actually cheer people on who don't support the same things you do. There is no reason to subjectively pull them down except for our own insecurities. We need everyone who has the passion to make the world a better place to take that passion and move forward, regardless of whether it is our own cause or not.

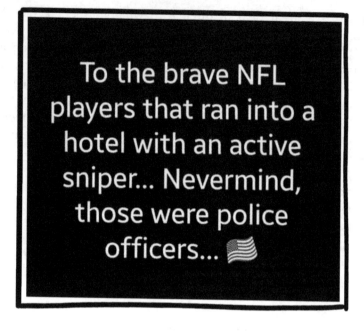

7.8 Cause shaming is one of the most common ways you will see protests being discredited. This meme is a 'They Don't Deserve Better Because...' meme that uses cause shaming by leveraging men that serve our country as a standard to discredit and shame others.

7.8 Cause Splitting

This is almost entirely owned by liberals, although it has good intentions. Progressives draw power to help others through empathy, but that empathy can also split us up. When we depart from a cause to support an even more niche faction inside of it, we have just added to the opposition for the larger change. It isn't that the niche is unimportant; it is that we have now added to the opposition for something we originally supported. Think about it as a protest being considered not inclusive enough for certain demographics or cultures, or even being looked at as too slow moving. The larger picture is sacrificed for smaller goals, which dramatically hinders the progress of the movement as a whole.

From a marketing viewpoint, cause splitting is a main reason progressives have major problems trying to get movements to work—because of the inner fighting about nuance. It is also why many who need education on the issue have problems understanding what specific change is actually desired, because from the outside the message is unclear. This creates a lack of consistency, which is bad marketing. To make any change happen, you have to be united and leverage KISS to be consistent with your message so others hear you. You are stronger together when you all reinforce one message than in small groups advocating for all kinds of nuanced things.

7.9 Radicals Do Not Represent a Movement

I shouldn't have to touch on this, but here goes. Single radicals don't represent a movement, but a pattern or a large group of radicals is a movement. A white supremacist march is a movement. A pattern of white men committing mass shootings is a movement. However, if you are going to cherry-pick one crazy guy as an example, you aren't helping anyone. The only way that crazy guy matters is if he has a following of people who are complicit to his rhetoric and he fits into a larger pattern.

7.10 An Entire Demographic May Not Stand Where You Assume

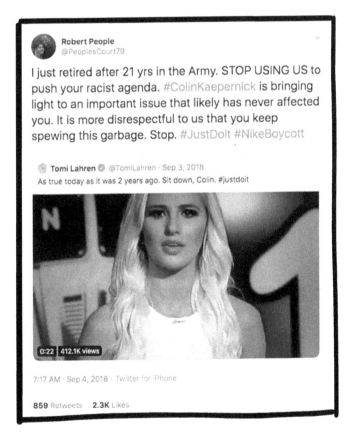

7.11 Don't assume an entire demographic stands where you think they do and don't leverage them for your own opinion. That is truly disrespectful. People are diverse and may not all stand where you assume they do.

We have all done this. And it is purely a projection of our own assumptions about a group of people. I remember heading towards the March for Our Lives, and I kept passing men in camo, hunting gear, and orange vests, which increased my anxiety. I envisioned these men yelling against us, with loaded weapons in public, threatening the children in the march. I based that assumption off the threats I saw posted online prior to the march. I swallowed my anxiety and pretended not to notice them; I was determined to march even if threatened by armed men.

And you know what happened? Nothing. The men in camo and blaze orange hunting gear were there in support of the children. They did not come armed. They came with signs saying, "Hunters for Common Sense Gun Control," and those blaze orange shirts said, "Hunters Against Being Shot." In my mind I had made it up that all gun owners were against common sense gun control, and it simply wasn't true. They are as varied as you and me, and I am sure many of them have children in school and would love to not worry about them being safe in a classroom.

I see people do this all the time with protests. They assume an entire demographic of people are on one side of the protest. An easy example is NFL players taking a knee during the national anthem. I can't tell you how many people I have seen screaming online about how this is disrespectful to our military. But our military is as diverse as our country, and you can't speak for all of them. Just as I assumed those in hunting gear were against common sense gun control, many people assume the entire military is against a protest made to end racial violence. It just isn't true. There are vets and active members of our military who are on both sides of the argument.

7.11 Racist and Hate Movements

> "In the end, we will remember not the words of our enemies, but the silence of our friends."
>
> - Martin Luther King Jr.

This section is short because there is no nuance I want to explain or any kind of marketing that you need to understand. Racists and racially charged hateful rhetoric should not be tolerated, and we should stand up to it. We shouldn't be complicit, silent, or tolerant. Our country has fought wars against these ideologies, and thousands of Americans have died to stop them. Being complicit/tolerant insults the sacrifices made to stop the spread of those ideologies. Being complicit/tolerant gives these beliefs your blessing and gives them a chance to continue to spread their message and grow their following. We can do better.

7.12 Renaming Causes For Comfort

Remember in elementary school (and even into adulthood) when kids would pick on each other by changing someone's name to something insulting to taunt them? I think about the movie *Never Been Kissed*, when the kids taunted Drew Barrymore's character with the nickname Josie 'Grossy.' We have grown up imprinted with the idea of renaming things we dislike through bullying culture.

> *"People have the right to call themselves whatever they like. That doesn't bother me. It's other people doing the calling that bothers me."*
>
> - Octavia E. Butler

I don't care if it is with the best intentions, I don't care if you are trying to be more inclusive, by changing the slogan of a protest to something you are more comfortable with, you are taking part in a bullying tactic. For example: you are not being supportive 'in your own way.' If someone wants you to say, "BLACK LIVES MATTER" and you change it to, "ALL LIVES MATTER," it is absolutely not the same thing, and it's not better because you have now made it more inclusive. You are not somehow being Switzerland and somehow not taking a side on this issue. At best you have taken a liberty with the cause that you were never given permission for and at worst you are mocking what the movement stands for and have signaled to others that you are completely against their cause.

I find this to be a super interesting form of trolling, because once someone rewords a protest, it goes viral by those who fail to find the words as to why the cause makes them uncomfortable. You would never see anyone reword a cause that isn't a political hot button issue. Why? Because that would make you an asshole. Think about it. You would never change The March of Dimes or Go Pink because that would be super disrespectful. Yet that is what is happening. Because it is a political issue, we often completely miss that the point of the movement is in the wording chosen for it.

By changing the slogan, people are often shaming the action they don't understand, even if their intentions are good. A perfect example of this was the viral post telling students to 'Walk Up and not Walk Out.' After the Parkland massacre where seventeen people tragically lost their lives, the students organized a national school walkout. The idea of the school walkout was to spur awareness. The absence of the students walking out of the classroom represented students whose seats are now empty due to gun violence in America. But the morning of the event a post went viral with the word 'out' crossed out of the slogan, and it was changed to 'Walk up.' By crossing out that word, you are visually telling people not to do something. The crossing out of the word means you do not support them. You do not support children who want action taken so they don't get shot in schools ... not cool, America. Then by changing it to 'Walk Up' you are now saying the kids can prevent this from happening.

If only these kids were nicer. If only they made the effort. Yeah ... that is horrible. It is no child's fault if they get shot and killed by a mass murderer when the adults have done nothing to prevent it. Many people explained they just supported people being nicer, and that is why they shared this post. But in one post they not only stood against the children calling on us to take action to prevent future shootings, but blamed them for not taking action appropriate to prevent future shootings. It is like blaming a rape victim for wearing clothes that you perceive were asking for it. If you look at it that way, it is actually shockingly toxic. It is all in how you look at it. And when you change a slogan you are doing more than making yourself comfortable.

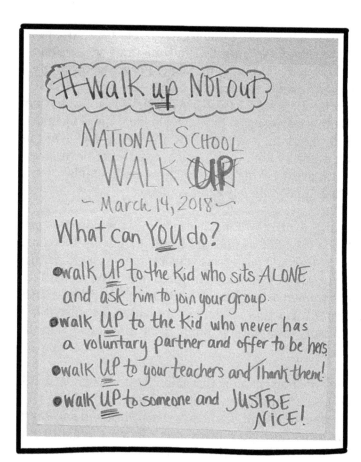

7.13 This image went insanely viral. And it is also insanely inappropriate when you think about it from the opposing viewpoint of the people who posted it thinking it was a nice gesture. Critiquing our children's behavior as some way their responsibility for getting shot while in school while adults do nothing is horrible to me and many people on the opposing side of this post.

CHAPTER 8

FINAL THOUGHTS

8.1 The Best and Worst Marketing Awards Go To...

The GOP has the best marketing in politics right now. They double down on what works and that is a perfect marketing strategy. They repeat statements that work over and over, and they do not break rank. All of this plays out brilliantly in an easily distracted culture where a meme wins over real conversation on topics. You don't need to read an article when someone calls it fake news. You know who your enemy is when they are always referred to with demeaning nicknames and innuendos to make it very clear. The appeals to fear and hatred also are hugely influential on the far right and have changed the direction of the GOP as a whole. The appeals to fear and hatred from the far right on all the information they spread (real or fake) leverages instinctive thinking and competitive victimhood to the point where facts and empathy have little sway on issues. The marketing is genius.

And the losers in the game of political marketing are the liberals. They cause split, they cause shame, and they absolutely fail when it comes to getting information out to stop propaganda from filling the information gap. Liberals need to stop infighting and focus on telling one message. Having all kinds of different messages doesn't work in a post-literate world. But it falls right in line with how progressives think. They don't care if they think something different than another progressive and they are not afraid to say it, because saying something new doesn't kick you out of the 'liberal club.' It does, however, make horrible communication and marketing. No one can figure out what you want if it keeps changing!

Progressives also need to start at the beginning with their messages. Too often they think everyone is on the same page and they don't address fears and misunderstandings. This helps no one. And I think this is arrogance on their part. They feel they are dumbing down the message, but in reality, if someone has never had a conversation about a topic, you have to start at the beginning.

8.2 Technology is only going to change faster and faster

I believe that the greatest power the Internet gave us was the power to share small ideas. In the past, you had to have a BIG idea to get it seen by a large number of people. A century ago we wrote personal letters, but to get information to a wider audience it would have had to be published in a book or in the newspaper. Now the distance a small idea has to travel to get to consumers has gotten shorter, with fewer gatekeepers to go through. We can now spread small ideas. And we can build on them fast.

> "We get scared 'cause we get old. We get scared of everything we didn't grow up with. It's what human beings do."
>
> -Gary Vaynerchuck

Things are moving faster and faster. Unfortunately, as easy as it is for good things to spread with this access to the masses, it also means bad things are easier to spread too. So we have to become better consumers and be savvier about what we are being marketed. We have to become vigilant about fact-checking instead of continuing to blame our responses to the content on everyone but ourselves. This is going to be especially vital for older generations[8.2.1] and those who claim they don't pay attention to politics as they are far more susceptible to malicious content.

> "The measure of intelligence is the ability to change."
>
> - Albert Einstein

There is a 24-hour Artificial Intelligence (AI) news anchor delivering news right now in China[8.2.2], and this is just the beginning. Soon AI will be used in everyday propaganda videos. The hate is going to get more technologically advanced, and if we can't recognize when we are being marketed to now, it will only get worse in the future. If we continue to be set in our ways and not change as technology changes, hate wins. I made one meme. Just one. And that one meme impacted the world. How many memes have you shared? What impact could you make if you took responsibility for what you post? It starts here. Time to change and be more vigilant consumers of information.

8.3 What Are You Supposed to Believe?

Marketing is supposed to make you feel something and act a certain way. Nowhere in this book did I warn against the marketing of happiness, joy, and spreading love for one another. Why? Because we all need more of that.

> *"I don't have to know you to love you."*
> - Cleo Wade

What are you watching? What memes do you agree with? Is the content you are consuming telling you someone is the enemy? Are they justifying treatment of someone worse than you would expect to be treated? Do they accuse people of something? Do they dehumanize someone? Are they repetitive and hateful? All of this matters because it is marketing hate and you need to be instantly skeptical when hate is the story you are being told upfront, because there is an agenda behind marketing hate, and you don't want to be a part of it. Pay attention to the content you are surrounding yourself with because it is changing your mind whether you think it is or not.

8.4 Time to take more responsibility

> *"It doesn't matter whose fault it is if something is broken, if it's your responsibility to fix it."*
> - Will Smith

Growing up in the Midwest, responsibility and integrity was a cornerstone of my daily life. It wasn't just being personally responsible and having integrity; being responsible meant going above and beyond to take care of others. I was taught that if you borrowed someone's car, you returned it with a full tank of gas. because even if you only drove it a couple miles that day, it was your responsibility to leave it better than it was before you borrowed it.

My grandmother was my role model for responsibility and integrity. She always set an extra plate at dinner and tried to fill the seat. Anyone who needed a hot meal could always get fed at Grandma Mary's house. My aunt was a dorm mother at the local college, and every holiday when the dorms would close and some of the students had nowhere to go, they had a hot holiday meal with my family. I don't remember a single holiday growing up without someone I didn't know at the table. But just because they weren't family, and their lack of somewhere to go wasn't our fault, it didn't mean it wasn't our responsibility to make sure they had somewhere to go. These kids were our kids and it didn't matter where in the world they came from, what language they spoke, or what they looked like.

My grandmother also gave dozens of people down on their luck a place to live in her home over the years. She opened her home, no questions asked, and she taught me what being a true follower of Christ looks like. She stood up for these people even when their families, who were supposed to protect them, wouldn't. And she always was the first person to call you on your bullshit if you were speaking badly of people. She would stand up for people who needed it most, no matter who they were. She always had the integrity to speak up and do the right thing, even if it wasn't her fault.

> *"...It has become increasingly apparent to me, that we all need to use our influence, whatever it may be, to help others."*
>
> - Ellen Page

When was the last time you stood up for someone who wasn't just like you? When was the last time you left something better than when it was given to you? With so much of our communication being done online I think we forget that we are all connected and we each are responsible for what it has become. We forget that it isn't just about us and our rights and our taxes and what makes us comfortable. And marketing has programmed us to think a blatant disregard for how our behavior impacts others is the way to get ahead in this world. Look at popular 'reality' tv shows with people sabotaging one another to get ahead, or the celebrity monarchies that behave monstrously yet maintain their wealth and power. It appears that success is purely about self-interest.

But that isn't how the real-world works. We all do better when we all do better. And working together will get you much farther than ever spending your time trying to sabotage others. And those shit show celebrity families with all the success and wild behavior have massive production teams to run their lives and get their shows produced. It is a huge team of people working together to create that illusion, and we have to remember that it is all marketing.

Because I am an Internet marketer, I see behind the curtain. I see all the deceptive and often sinister marketing tactics that take us away from truth and being good to one another. I hope I helped you see through some of these tactics. This is me filling up the tank. If you want to talk more about any idea you read in this book you can reach me at KatherineYoungCreative.com, I will set out an extra plate for you. This book is my attempt to remind us all that the responsibility of showing up as your best self with integrity shouldn't change because of marketing. It shouldn't change because it is online. Your actions are your actions no matter when or where they take place. It is time to do better.

GLOSSARY

These are common terms I use in this book. Sometimes I use marketing lingo and I want to make sure we are all on the same page.

Algorithm (noun)
An algorithm is a process which computers, websites, and applications figure out how to present information automatically based on how we have used them in the past.

Consumers (noun)
Consumers are anyone online who sees this content online. Being a consumer doesn't mean you have to buy something. Your attention is enough to make you a consumer.

Divisive Content (noun)
A post online that is made primarily to point the finger at a group or individual to let them know they are in the wrong according to your subjective opinion, more so than to promote a cause you care about. You may think your post isn't divisive, but it usually takes an opposing viewpoint to see it in the context it was truly meant for. These posts put negativity into the world instead of positivity when discussing political topics and let people know they are your enemy and you are against them.

Hashtag (noun)
A hashtag refers to the actual symbol used plus the words behind it without any spaces. On social media these are used as easy ways to find connected information. If you use a hashtag you add what you are saying to a bigger conversation about the topic and help people find what you have to say. Examples: #MeToo #BlackLivesMatter #StopSucking

Like (noun and verb)
A like is the actual act of giving a post a designation of approval usually by clicking a small icon of a heart or a thumbs-up. It is how you can easily tell someone you saw what they posted.

Marketers/Marketing (noun and verb)
Marketing or marketers are any action/person/organization that is trying to elicit a response of some kind. You don't have to be paid to be marketing something. You simply want to garner a response.

Meme (noun)
A meme is a humorous or impactful image, video, piece of text, etc., that is copied (often with slight variations) and shared rapidly by Internet users.

Post (noun and verb)
A post is anything you share online. It can be just typing or sharing another form of media. It can also refer to the actual act of sharing. You are the poster if you post something.

Share (verb)
When you spread a post by showing it to other people online. It comes from you when they see it.

Social media, online, and the Internet (noun)
I am also going to use the words pretty interchangeably. This is because I think of social media as just the current condition of the Internet. There really isn't any place that you can't be heard if you want to be heard online.

Scream/Yell (verb)
I am referring to the way your typed words are coming across online when someone else sees the content you posted in their feed. Even if it is just words they might be read as if you are yelling at someone because of the way it uses aggressive language.

Troll (noun and verb)
A troll is someone who wants attention for their thoughts online and goes about it by bullying, being divisive, and spreading misinformation to fit their agenda. They create most memes and are defined by their acts of online hatred. A troll can be anyone who displays this kind of behavior.

Trope (noun)
You can think of a trope as a stereotype. When people talk about tropes, they usually refer to an idea that is very well-known and over-used in a negative way that lacks actual authenticity. Tropes are usually leaned on when someone lacks actual knowledge on the subject they are talking about.

Viral (adjective)
This means a post spreads extremely fast and extremely far by people online sharing it.

RESOURCES

Not all the resources listed here are referenced in the text. If I used them for research and think they will be helpful I included them for readers to do their own research.

The Art of War by Sun Tzu

"The Billion-Dollar Disinformation Campaign to Reelect the President" by *The Atlantic*
https://www.theatlantic.com/magazine/archive/2020/03/the-2020-disinformation-war/605530

"Blue Feed, Red Feed" by *Wall Street Journal*
https://graphics.wsj.com/blue-feed-red-feed/

"Celebrities & Politics" by Mayim Bialik
https://youtu.be/f9Ben1SB4aY

"Dangers of Nostalgizing" by Stephanie Coontz
https://youtu.be/IyGDH0CuE6E

"The danger of a single story" by Chimamanda Ngozi Adichie
https://www.ted.com/talks/chimamanda_ngozi_adichie_the_danger_of_a_single_story

The Evolution of Thought: Why We Think the Way We Do
by Roger Bourke White Jr.

Fact-checking websites:
FactCheck.org
PolitiFact
Snopes
Washington Post Fact Checker
NPR Fact Checker

Factfulness: Ten Reasons We're Wrong About the World--and Why Things Are Better Than You Think by Hans Rosling

Fake News: Separating Truth from Fiction by Michael Miller

Girl, Wash Your Face: Stop Believing the Lies about Who You Are So You Can Become Who You Were Meant to Be
by Rachel Hollis

Girl, Stop Apologizing: A Shame-free Plan for Embracing and Achieving Your Goals by Rachel Hollis

The Great Hack by Netflix

Image search: (reverse image search) images.google.com

I Am Malala: The Girl Who Stood Up for Education and Was Shot by the Taliban by Malala Yousafzai

"I grew up in the Westboro Baptist Church. Here's why I left" by Megan Phelps-Roper https://www.ted.com/talks/megan_phelps_roper_i_grew_up_in_the_ westboro_baptist_church_here_s_why_i_left

An Illustrated Book of Bad Arguments by Ali Almossawi

Media Bias Charts: https://www.adfontesmedia.com/ https://www.allsides.com/media-bias/media-bias-chart

The Moment of Lift: How Empowering Women Changes the World by Melinda Gates

The Obstacle is the Way: The Ancient Art of Turning Adversity to Advantage by Ryan Holiday

The Opposite of Hate by Sally Kohn.

The Power of Habit: Why We Do What We Do in Life and Business by Charles Duhigg

Southern Poverty Law Center: https://www.splcenter.org/

Representative contact app Resistbot: Text RESIST to 50409 to contact your representation

The Righteous Mind: Why Good People Are Divided by Politics and Religion by Jonathan Haidt

"A royal obsession with black magic started Europe's most brutal witch hunts" by *National Geographic* https://www.nationalgeographic.com/history/magazine/2019/09-10/scotland-witch-hunts/

"Someone I Know Loves This Fake News" by Katherine Young
https://www.katherineyoungcreative.com/blog/2017/9/26/someone-i-know-loves-this-fake-news

Talking Across the Divide: How to Communicate with People You Disagree with and Maybe Even Change the World by Justin Lee

Talking to Strangers: What We Should Know about the People We Don't Know by Malcolm Gladwell

"That Uplifting Tweet You Just Shared? A Russian Troll Sent It" by *Rolling Stone*

This Is Marketing by Seth Godin

"Trump Weaponizes Victimhood to Defend Kavanaugh" - *Between the Scenes* by *The Daily Show* with Trevor Noah
https://youtu.be/4LZ3P1sv9jE

What Unites Us: Reflections on Patriotism by Dan Rather

Where to Begin: A Small Book About Your Power to Create Big Change in Our Crazy World by Cleo Wade

White Fragility: Why It's So Hard for White People to Talk About Racism by Robin DiAngelo

BIBLIOGRAPHY

All memes and images in this book not created by the author specifically for this book were posted publicly by people known by the author. If you find yourself thinking "No normal person would actually post that," think again. The links cited here were done to guarantee them anonymity. When the original link would lead back to any of their personal social profiles I either referenced the images back only to the social platform it was posted on or cited the image or a similar image found elsewhere online.

1.4.1
Angry Hillary meme + author created layout and text / imgflip /Accessed June 14, 2018 / imgflip.com/memetemplate/84139500/Angry-Hillary-Clinton

1.4.2
Mike Pence RFRA meme + author created layout and text / imgflip /Accessed June 18, 2019 / imgflip.com/memetemplate/32497823/Mike-Pence-RFRA

1.4.3
Fake News Cycle infographic made by author

1.5.1
Girls' Life vs. Boys' Life digital image / facebook / August 31, 2016 / facebook.com/mattjfrye/posts/10209018357749474

1.5.2
Girls' Life Cover redo comparison digital image / Katherine Young Creative / September 6, 2016 / katherineyoungcreative.com/blog/2016/9/7/girls-life-we-need-to-do-better

1.5.3
Video screen grab of TODAY morning segment / TODAY / September 21, 2016 / today.com/parents/girls-life-vs-boys-life-cover-comparison-leaves-us-shaking-t103112

1.5.4
Suck it GIRLS' LIFE screengrab of social post including reach metrics / facebook / September 8, 2016 / facebook.com/522823434498903 posts/1050705035044071?s=163900871&sfns=mo

1.5.5
Fake Jerry Jones quote meme digital image / Katherine Young Creative / September 30, 2017 / https://www.katherineyoungcreative.com/blog/2017/9/26/someone-i-know-loves-this-fake-news

2.2
Life is Short meme digital image / facebook / September 2, 2019 / facebook.com

2.3
People Offended by Everything meme digital image / facebook / March 16, 2019 / facebook.com

2.4
Lori McAllen screengrabbed statement meme digital image / The Orgonian / June 21, 2018 / www.oregonlive.com/pacific-northwest-news/2018/06/oregon_dmv_employees_purported.html

2.7
Parroting graphic was created by the author

2.9
Screengrabbed tweets from J. K . Rowling / Twitter / July 3, 208/
twitter.com/jk_rowling/status/1014290773934792704

2.11.2
Image screengrabbed from post of viral article shaming women for being on their phones
/ Sports on Tap /Accessed September 20, 2018 / sontlive.com /2018/08/20/listen-to-
the-announcers-reactions-of-sorority-girls-ignoring-the-baseball-game/

2.11.2
List of social media rules graphic was created by the author

3.1.1
"The DNA of Viral Content" / *The Guardian* / September 15, 2014 /
https://www.theguardian.com/media/2014/sep/15/the-dna-of-viral-content

3.15
Trump pussy comment explained meme digital image / Twitter /Accessed October 11,
2016 / www.twitter.com

3.15
Trump tweet digital image / Twitter /December 31, 2016 / twitter.com/
realDonaldTrump

3.29
Fake Pepsi meme digital image / Facebook /Accessed July 19, 2018 / www.facebook.com

3.30.2
Corporations Funding meme digital image / Facebook /Accessed May 5, 2019 /
www.facebook.com

3.31
Mollie Tibbett #buildthewall meme digital image / Facebook /Accessed August 22, 2018 /
www.facebook.com

3.37
Politically incorrect faux patriotism meme digital image / Twitter /Accessed January 21,
2020 / https://twitter.com/rockonohio

3.37
Mocking aggressively faux patriotism meme digital image / Reddit /Accessed July 21,
2019 / https://www.reddit.com/r/PoliticalHumor/duplicates/cferba/this_is_america_
love_it_or_leave_it_snowflake/

3.42.1
"Re: I want to meet *insert name*" e-mail digital image / from info@barackobama.com
/sent October 13, 2010

3.42.2
"I'm going all in" e-mail digital image / from contact@victory.donaldtrump.com /sent
October 24, 2018

3.42.2.1
"Matching-donation fundraisers can be harmfully dishonest" / Effective Altruism Forum /
December 15, 2011 (updated on: July 25, 2016) https://forum.effectivealtruism.org/posts/
a2gYyTnAP36TxqdQp/matching-donation-fundraisers-can-be-harmfully-dishonest

3.42.3
"Announcing the Year in Hope" e-mail digital image / from info@obama.org /sent December 19, 2019

3.42.4
"Officially Impeached" e-mail digital image / from contact@victory.donaldtrump.com / sent December 19, 2019

4.1
Text conversation digital image / imessages /Accessed January 3, 2020 / Texts provided by author

4.3.1
Donald Trump Jr. Racist Skittles tweet meme digital image / Twitter /Accessed June 17, 2018 / https://twitter.com/DonaldTrumpJr

4.3.2
False Analogy Comparison chart created by author

4.4
John vs. Juan meme screengrab digital image / Facebook / Accessed June 17, 2018 / Facebook.com

4.5
Shaming Unpatriot Parking meme digital image / Facebook /Accessed July 5, 2018 / https://facebook.com

4.8.1
Barack Obama tweet meme digital image / Snopes /Accessed March 16, 2019 / https://www.snopes.com/fact-check/barack-obama-grocery-tweet/

4.8.2
Donald Trump *People Magazine* meme digital image / Snopes /Accessed March 16, 2019 / https://www.snopes.com/fact-check/1998-trump-people-quote/

4.9
Hillary Clinton with Osama bin Laden comparison meme digital image / Politifact /Accessed Sept 2, 2019 / https://www.politifact.com/facebook-fact-checks/statements/2019/nov/05/viral-image/image-hillary-clinton-and-osama-bin-laden-doctored/

4.10
Fake Girl Hillary meme / Snopes / Accessed January 27, 2018 / https://www.snopes.com/fact-check/hillary-clinton-freed-child-rapist-laughed-about-it/

4.11.1
Hillary Hates Farmers meme digital image / Facebook /Accessed September 17, 2017 / https://www.facebook.com/sandra.hartle

4.11.2
Tax Payer Money tweet digital image / Twitter /Accessed August 29, 2018 / https://twitter.com/realmatmolina

4.11.3
Job Growth tweet and tweet response digital image / Facebook /Accessed August 8, 2018 / https://www.facebook.com/

4.12.1
Pick Your Poison meme digital image / mem.me /Accessed September 2, 2019 / https://me.me/t/pick-your-poison

4.12.2
Racist Saint vs. Sinner meme digital image / Facebook /Accessed September 2, 2019 / https://www.facebook.com/

4.12.3
Don't Deserve Better meme digital image / Facebook /Accessed October 31, 2018 / https://www.facebook.com/

4.12 4
Don't Deserve Better Military meme digital image / Facebook /Accessed October 31, 2018 / https://www.facebook.com/

4.13
Ace Ventura gif meme digital image / Facebook /Accessed September 2, 2019 / https://www.facebook.com/

4.14
Amazon Burning tweet meme digital image / Twitter / Accessed August 21, 2019 / https://twitter.com/damongameau

4.15
Apples vs. Oranges meme digital image / Reddit / Accessed January 28, 2020 / https://www.reddit.com/r/facepalm/comments/7jmycb/theyre_different_medals/

4.16
Mutually Exclusive Myth image comparison meme digital image / Facebook / Accessed March 4, 2019 / https://www.facebook.com/

4.17
Flip Flops Product digital image / *Business Insider* /Accessed September 2, 2019 / www.businessinsider.com/president-trump-flip-flops-made-from-tweets-2018-12

4.18
Wrong Kid Article post digital image / posted on Facebook / Accessed February 18, 2019 / https://www.facebook.com/

4.19
Fat Women Marching meme digital image / Facebook / Accessed April 3, 2019 / https://www.facebook.com/

4.20
Kids at the Border post meme digital image / Facebook / Accessed October 31, 2018 / https://www.facebook.com/

4.22
Brett Kavanaugh Conservative Opinion meme / Pinterest / July 13, 2018/ pinterest.com/jennifla79/my-body-my-choice

4.24
Image of Dr. Joe Medicine Crow turned into a meme digital image / Accessed via Facebook / Accessed October 31, 2018 / Original image made into meme: https://www.flickr.com/photos/63339942@N00/2531983077

4.25
Jewish Erasure Islamophobia meme digital image / Accessed via Facebook /Accessed September 2, 2019 / https://www.facebook.com/ with false information noted at: https://www.snopes.com/fact-check/holocaust-teaching-ban-uk/

4.26
#InsertCityNameHere meme digital image created by the author

4.27.1
Child and Junk Food meme digital image / Twitter / Accessed March 4, 2018 / https://twitter.com/TrutherUfo/status/969682912839946240

4.27.2
Fake Kurt Cobain Quote meme digital image / imgur / Accessed February 2, 2019 / https://imgur.com/r/nirvana/3R7CQGW

4.27.3
Bush Dancing with Wounded Warrior post digital image / Facebook / Accessed September 2, 2019 / https://www.facebook.com/Ibleedredwhiteandblue/posts/how-many-people-know-that-president-bush-hosts-a-few-wounded/834289016620123/

4.27.4
Donald Trump Name Calling tweet digital image / Twitter / Accessed January 27, 2020 / https://twitter.com/realDonaldTrump/status/1221079753760833536

4.27.5
Muslim Prayer Curtain meme digital image / Snopes / Accessed January 13, 2020 / https://www.snopes.com/fact-check/muslim-prayer-curtain-white-house/

4.27.6
Combination Presidents and Curtains digital image of created by author / Google Images / Accessed January 18, 2020 / https://images.app.goo.gl/ja9AFLwZKf7AazLc6, https://images.app.goo.gl/RUD3xVTt3VxV7JxP7, https://images.app.goo.gl/HWdaiB7Lxz6vjzN87, https://images.app.goo.gl/us48h65fm5gTC54J8

4.27.7
Gun Owner Victimhood Without Facts meme digital image / Facebook / Accessed December 11, 2019 / https://www.facebook.com/christopherfferry/photos/rifles-killed-less-than-300-people-last-year-heroin-killed-over-70000-but-if-you/733703823766379/

6.4.1
#HB2 Transgender tweet digital image / Twitter / Accessed March 27, 2016 / twitter.com/JayShef/status/712845760287494144

6.4.2
Cartoon of Troll in Information Gap created by author

6.5
Classic troll account photos archive digital image / Facebook / Accessed September 1, 2019 / facebook.com/sandra.hartle/photos

6.11.1
Celebrities Who Should Move to Canada meme digital image / Facebook / Accessed October 31, 2018 / https://www.facebook.com/

6.11.2
"Celebrities & Politics" / YouTube / Accessed June 23, 2018 / https://youtu.be/f9Ben1SB4aY

7.1.1
Infographic of bell curve made by author

7.1.2
Infographic of steps to marketing made by author

7.3
Author at the 2017 Women's March / January 21, 2017 / Saint Paul, MN State Capital

7.11
Military Service tweet rebuking Tomi Lahren tweet digital image / Twitter / Accessed January 30, 2020 / twitter.com/PeoplesCourt79/status/1036951378818682882

7.13
Walk Up Not Out Viral School Teacher post digital image / ABC News / Accessed March 16, 2019/ https://abcnews.go.com/US/News/middle-school-teacher-encourages-students-walk-walk/story?id=53738732

7.5.1
"10 Things You May Not Know About Martin Luther King Junior" / History.com / Accessed February 15, 2020/https://www.history.com/news/10-things-you-may-not-know-about-martin-luther-king-jr

7.5.2
"Until 1975, 'Sexual Harassment' Was the Menace With No Name" / History.com / Accessed February 15, 2020/ https://www.history.com/news/until-1975-sexual-harassment-was-the-menace-with-no-name

8.2.1
"Less than you think: Prevalence and predictors of fake news dissemination on Facebook" / *Science Advances* / Accessed February 15, 2020/ https://advances.sciencemag.org/content/5/1/eaau4586.full

8.2.2
"The World's First AI News Anchor has gone Live in China" / CNBC.com / Accessed February 15, 2020/ https://www.cnbc.com/2018/11/09/the-worlds-first-ai-news-anchor-has-gone-live-in-china.html

ACKNOWLEDGMENTS

Thank you to creatives I admire who lead the way by using their art and creativity to stand up for others and highlight political issues that matter. You inspired me to use my creativity intentionally to make a contribution to topics I care about.

Luvvie Ajayi Jones, Mayim Bialik, Danielle Colby, Felicia Day, Holly Exley, Jessica Hische, Rachel Hollis, Debbie Millman, Ellen Page, Cat Polivoda, Amy Schumer, Johnathan Van Ness, Gary Vaynerchuck, James Victore, Cleo Wade, Jack White, Reese Witherspoon, and Wil Wheaton

Thank you to self-published authors on YouTube (authortubers) who put out free content in all forms to help viewers publish their first books. I was able to write and publish this book by learning from you all.

Bethany Anyatazadeh, Sara Cannon | Heart Breathings, Natalia Leigh, Mandi Lynn, Kristen Martin, Jenna Moreci | Writing with Jenna Moreci Joanna Penn | The Creative Penn, & Dale L. Roberts | Self-Publishing with Dale

And ast but not least, thank you to my Beta Readers who took the time to give me their thoughts and send final edits before I sent this book out into the world. This book wouldn't be possible without you.

Jessica Ault, Amber S. Drummer-Woods, Laura Hann, Somer Hartman, Lindsay Kamakahi, Joelle Oliver, Levi B. Powell, Kris Rossow, Jessica Sievers, Kari Strickland, and Alex Van Eeckhout

ABOUT THE AUTHOR

Katherine is from a small town of less than 15,000 people in North Dakota. Growing up she never thought of the people around her as liberal or conservative. Her grandmother was her hero and the town matriarch and was known for standing up to people and saying what needed to be said and doing what needed to be done. Katherine has always tried to live up to her grandmother's example, which would now be considered very progressive even if she didn't know that as a child.

Katherine attended college for graphic design and went to work for the Walt Disney Company after college. There she learned from the best of the best and began running large social media accounts. She has been doing design and social media marketing professionally for more than a decade. She has created internationally viral content that has been featured by *The Huffington Post*, *TODAY*, Minnesota Public Radio, and many more. She currently works in nonprofit, supporting libraries and education.

Visit KatherineYoungCreative.com to learn more about Katherine.

If you enjoyed this book the best way you can help support the author and get this book into the hands of more people is to leave a review on Amazon or Goodreads.

CPSIA information can be obtained
at www.ICGtesting.com
Printed in the USA
LVHW012012270521
688708LV00011B/499